Crossing the Line

Crossing the Line

Immigrants, Economic Integration, and Drug Enforcement on the U.S.-Mexico Border

Tom Barry
with **Harry Browne** *and* **Beth Sims**

No. 3 in The U.S.-Mexico Series

Resource Center Press
Albuquerque, New Mexico

First Edition, 1994

No. 3 in The U.S.-Mexico Series

Production/design by John Hawley/Resource Center Press

Resource Center Press
Box 4506 / Albuquerque, New Mexico 87196

ISBN: 0-911213-46-5

Acknowledgments

This book would not have been possible without the direct contributions of many friends and colleagues. The staff of the Resource Center formed the foundation that allowed the book to take shape. Although all staff members helped at one time or another, especially important was the research assistance by Ricardo Hernández, Erik Leaver, Edith Sánchez, Laura Sheridan, and Steve Whitman; the administrative and personal support offered by executive director Debra Preusch; and the publications skills of production manager John Hawley.

Vital in detecting errors, correcting misconceptions, and offering important insights were the following area experts who commented on parts of the manuscript and shared their information: Roderic Camp, C. Richard Bath, Paul Ganster, Rodolfo O. de la Garza, Antonio González, Peter Lupsha, Philip Martin, Oscar Martínez, Stephen Mumme, Fred Schellenberg, and Peter Schey. Finally we gratefully acknowledge the financial support of the John D. and Catherine T. MacArthur Foundation, North Shore Unitarian Universalist Veatch Program, Threshold Foundation, United Church of Christ, and the Max and Anna Levinson Foundation our U.S.-Mexico project. Also important were the many individual contributors and patrons of the Resource Center.

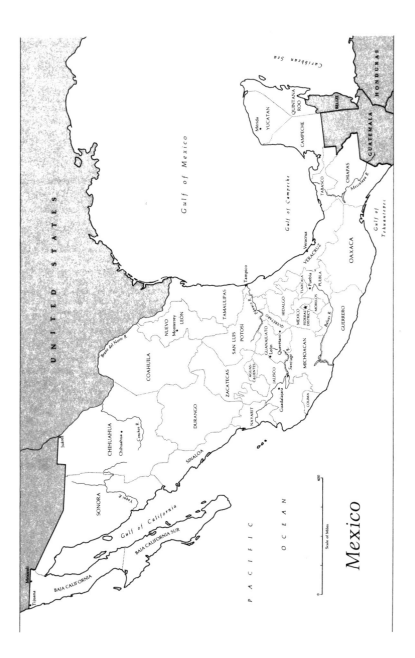

Mexico

Contents

Chapter 5:
Calling in the Troops

Chapter 6:
Manufacturing on the Margin

Chapter 7:
Dual Development:
The Neverending Promise

References

Appendix:
Selected Border Organizations

Where North and South Meet

The border between the United States and Mexico is an arbitrary line drawn straight through desert sage and sand. The Rio Grande defines more than 1,200 miles of this 1,952-mile line, but from El Paso-Ciudad Juárez to San Diego-Tijuana the international division has no natural dimension.

To cross this line is to enter not only a different nation but also another part of the world. Immigrants from Latin America leave the third world and underdevelopment for an encounter with the "developed" world. The U.S.-Mexico border is the dividing line between the South and the North, the boundary that separates colony from imperium, desperation from hope. At no other international border are the contrasts so striking. The desert is no different, the sky is the same impenetrable blue. But from one side to the other, the human landscape is foreign.

All international borders are at once fascinating and disconcerting. They awaken and challenge one's sense of national identity. But it is not the contrasting cultures, the differences between political systems, or even the sudden change in language that makes crossing the U.S.-Mexico line so shocking. Instead, it is the experience of passing so rapidly between economic worlds. The line is the edge of a third world society that reaches ever farther south, beyond Juárez to the teeming *barrios* of Mexico City and into the Central American isthmus. The line divides the industrial North from the misery of the Southern Hemisphere. Crossing north to south, paved streets, auto insurance, and the American dream are left behind for a part of the world—the largest part—where one-room hovels, economic misery, and the lack of basic public services are the norm.

The dividing line is stark and unmistakable. But it is not impermeable. In fact, its ability to keep the two worlds apart has steadily diminished. Those living in the borderlands, that stretch of territory paralleling the boundary on either side, have long recognized and exploited the porous border. Many have family on both sides, and the respective economies, although dramatically different, have always been interdependent. Crossing the line is as routine as visiting relatives, shopping, or going to work.

Most U.S. citizens, however, have no personal or economic links south of the border. The U.S.-Mexico boundary underlined their privilege while isolating them from the political turmoil and economic desperation of their southern neighbors. Mexico, a nation of eighty-six million, was part of an unknown world that did not touch their lives.

Yet the borderlands have been slowly inching northward. No longer are immigrant foreign workers confined to the agriculture of the Southwest; over the past two decades they have become an integral part of the low-paid service sector throughout the United States. Mexican boys are selling flowers on the streets of New York City, Salvadorans are working in the restaurants of Washington, D.C., and Mexican women are serving as maids and nannies from Portland to Atlanta. Latin Americans are of course not the only foreigners crossing into the United States, but it is the new wave of Spanish speakers predominantly from Mexico, Central America, and the Caribbean that has alerted U.S. citizens to the fact that the dividing line between the United States and Latin America is no longer so clearly demarcated.

The cross-border movement has by no means been in one direction. The self-proclaimed Manifest Destiny of the United States justified the habitual expansion of U.S. boundaries in the nineteenth century. Recognizing that the days of filibusters and colonialism were over, twentieth-century America relied on its new economic might backed by an open-door policy of free trade to push its way past foreign borders in industrial capitalism's aggressive search for new markets and raw materials. With the United States the undisputed capitalist center at the close of World War II, U.S.-based transnational corporations began crisscrossing international boundary lines with increasing ease.

The globalization of production has been developing since the late 1950s, and has involved Mexico since the mid-1960s. With the 1965 creation of the Border Industrialization Program, the export-oriented maquila sector was born in Mexico. Relocating to sites with cheaper work forces has been a manufacturing tradition in the United States. At first, firms in the industrial belt looked to the nonunionized southern and southwestern states. Hoping to boost wider economic development, Sun Belt states competed with each other by offering relocating companies special tax exemptions, free warehouse facilities, and unorganized work forces. Crossing state lines to find more profitable manufacturing locations readied the U.S. corporate sector for international border-hopping. Tennessee or New Mexico could compete with Connecticut and Michigan but not with the dollar-an-hour wages of the Mexican borderlands and other foreign locations.

Many businesses and free trade proponents regard the border line as part of the bottom line of company balance sheets. Crossing the international border is essential to keeping U.S. firms competitive and profitable, they argue. Free trade and capital's ability—indeed its right—to seek higher return across international borders have become part of the new ideology of global capitalism. National borders, the public welfare, and governments all must align themselves with this imperative of global trade and investment. There is a mathematical logic and beauty to this ideology of the global bottom line that does not leave room for consideration of nonbusiness questions concerning social equity and environmental sustainability.

In many ways, the line separating the southern United States and Mexico is a metaphor for the economic future of America. In attempting to bridge this international divide, U.S. and Mexican citizens alike face choices and challenges that arise from living in an increasingly global economy and society.

Asymmetry and Interdependence in the Borderlands

Geography brings the United States and Mexico together. It is along their common border that many of the challenges that face the two nations are most acutely felt. The society and economy of the borderlands reflect historic tensions and divisions between the two nations. At the same time, the increasing interdependence of the neighboring countries is most apparent in the border region. Just as obvious is the asymmetry that characterizes binational relations. Although many U.S. border cities are deeply dependent upon their larger Mexican twins for retail trade, the disparity between the two countries in wealth, welfare, and productive infra-structure is obvious to anyone traveling through the borderlands.

At the border the two societies stand side by side, and their economic interactions highlight the benefits and problems of having a poor nation rub shoulders with a wealthier one. As the barriers to foreign imports and investment fall, the border is less a dividing line between two economies and more a wall between two societies. For the most part, it serves to obstruct northbound migration while raising few barriers for U.S. citizens wanting to visit or live in Mexico. Retirees and other snowbirds looking for a warm climate and a less expensive place to retire have established expatriate enclaves throughout Mexico. But there is no corresponding legal freedom of movement for those seeking jobs and new lives north of the border.

The borderlands are the place where one best sees the problems of crossing the great economic and social divide between the two neighbors. Here the two societies are meshing, and economic integration is a daily occurrence. But the border is also a battleground where the U.S. authorities have mobilized their defenses against the advances of northbound immigration and narcotics flow.

Defining the Border

Politics, war, and economic expansion carved the borderline that separates Mexico and the United States. At first no fences or opposing flags marked this line dividing the largely uncharted and unpopulated region now known as the U.S.-Mexico borderlands. Today, however, the border is no longer just a mapmaker's creation. It is firmly fixed by concrete channels, steel walls, barbed wire, boundary markers, cattle fences, and the understanding that life is decidedly different on the other side.

The secession from Mexico of the Lone Star Republic of Texas in 1836 signaled the beginning of the erosion of Mexico's northern territories. A decade later the Treaty of Guadalupe Hidalgo, which ended the Mexican-American War of 1846-48, reduced Mexico by nearly half. This new territory eventually became the province of eight new U.S. states.[1]

Superior U.S. military power proved decisive in drawing the new international boundary, but the border line was also the result of financial dealings between a wealthy, expansionist nation and an unscrupulous leader of a poor one. As compensation for its severed lands, Mexico under General Santa Ana received fifteen million dollars from Washington in 1848 and another ten million dollars for the Gadsden Purchase in 1853. The Gadsden Purchase, which placed a strip of land along the bottom of what is now Arizona and New Mexico in U.S. hands, was the last major alteration in the international border.

For 1,254 miles the international boundary follows the Rio Grande on its path southeast from El Paso del Norte (now the site of El Paso and Ciudad Juárez) to the Gulf of Mexico. Being shallow and intermittent in parts, the Rio Grande does not, however, form an effective barrier between the two nations.[2] West of the Rio Grande (known in Mexico as the Río Bravo del Norte) no natural features define the border, with the brief exception of the Colorado River. Until the International Boundary Commission got to work placing stone boundary markers, the border was just a phantom line through the Chihuahuan and Sonoran deserts. From the Rio Grande to the Pacific the border stretches 698 miles, including a twenty-four-mile jog along the Colorado River. Altogether—from the Gulf of Mexico to the Pacific Ocean—the U.S.-Mexico international boundary extends 1,952 miles (3,141 km).

The chief difficulty in maintaining the boundary has been the willful Río Bravo del Norte. Silt accumulations in the shallow channel have caused the river to overflow its banks and establish new channels. In an attempt to solve the boundary problems caused by the meandering river, the two nations signed an agreement in 1889 that the boundary would follow the center of the normal channels of the Rio Grande and the Colorado River. The most serious territorial dispute that arose because of the shifting banks of the Rio Grande occurred in 1911 where the river splits El Paso and Juárez. It took more than a half-century of negotiations and legal action to determine the boundary line.[3] To keep Mexico south of the river and the United States north, and thereby avoid continuing territorial disputes, the U.S. Army Corps of Engineers in the 1960s "rectified" the erratic Rio Grande by constraining it within concrete channels as it turns southeast at El Paso.

Other than a scattering of missions, forts, and ranches, what are now the borderlands were sparsely populated in the mid-1800s. The Mexican population immediately adjacent to what would be defined as the border was largely confined to southeast

Texas and southern California. The vast arid stretch of desert and mountains in between these two regions was the domain of various Indian tribes.[4]

A series of twin border towns emerged gradually in the last half of the nineteenth century. Some had their origins as frontier military posts or old Spanish *ranchos* while others developed primarily to satisfy the demands of north-south trade. In a few cases, Mexican refugees from what had suddenly become part of the United States created new towns such as Nuevo Laredo on the southern side of the new international boundary.

Slowly the border region began taking shape. From a line traced through empty horizons, the border became a zone of development. Established as a boundary to keep two nations apart, over time the border drew the neighboring economies and societies together. The centers of this mutual attraction are the interdependent twin cities that serve as the hubs for the expanding border economy.[5]

In the late 1880s the newly laid railroads resulted in a surge of new settlers in the U.S. southwest. In 1887 alone, Southern California received 120,000 Anglo settlers, overwhelming the some 12,000 Mexican-Americans then living in the area.[6] The Prohibition era (1918-1933) and the associated cross-border vice business sparked the initial boom in many Mexican border towns. Later, the war economy of the 1940s and in particular the siting of new U.S. military bases in such border towns as El Paso and San Diego greatly boosted economic development along the border.

Beginning in the 1940s, the Mexican government stimulated development in northern Mexico with programs to expand irrigated agriculture in the northern states of Sinaloa, Tamaulipas, Baja California, Chihuahua, and Baja California. Similarly, agricultural development in southern California, particularly in the Imperial Valley, sparked economic and population growth in the borderlands. Another major stimulus to the expansion of the border population, particularly on the Mexican side, was the Bracero Program (1942-1964), a binational program that brought Mexican workers to the United States. Although the program attracted workers mainly from Mexico's interior, it sparked new waves of illegal migration northward into the United States. During times when jobs were difficult to find and when the program ended, thousands of workers retreated to the Mexican border cities.

Concerned that the United States would further encroach on its territory and society, it has long been the policy of the Mexican government to encourage migration to its northern borderlands.[7] Both in keeping with this policy and as a way to provide employment to returning *braceros*, the government created the Border Industrialization Program in the 1960s. The opening of the nation's northern frontier to export-oriented factories called maquiladoras (or maquilas), and the parallel development of the U.S. Sun Belt combined to foster economic and population growth in the borderlands in the post-World War II period.

There is little confusion about where one nation ends and the other begins, but a definition of the borderlands region is more problematic. Certainly the fourteen twin cities that straddle the border are included, although there is some debate about whether San Diego is really a border city since its economic center lies seventeen miles from Tijuana. Proud of their border home, El Paso residents assert that their historic city is the largest U.S. border town—not the pretentious San Diego. Not too long ago there were few who really cared about how far north or south the borderlands extended. But with recent national attention—and the prospect of new business and increased federal spending—the borderlands debate has heated up.

In Mexico the borderlands have generally been defined two ways: The broad definition includes the entirety of the six northern states, while the narrow definition refers only to a zone extending about thirteen miles south of the border to the customs checkpoints or encompassing the thirty-five *municipios* or municipalities that parallel the border.[8] Generally, when Mexicans speak of the *frontera norte* (northern border) or of the *fronterizos* they are referring to this narrow strip along the border and the people who live there. But *el norte* in Mexico refers to all six border states—Tamaulipas, Nuevo León, Coahuila, Chihuahua, Sonora, and Baja California—as well as Durango and Sinaloa, and sometimes even Zacatecas.[9]

In the United States there is no official border zone that hugs the boundary and is subject to special customs regulations as in Mexico. Unlike the Mexican side, all customs stations are at the port of entries, although the U.S. Border Patrol has inspection stations as far as seventy-five miles from the border. In the 1970s the Southwest Border Regional Commission developed a definition based on the twenty-five counties that skirt the border.[10] Another definition has the borderlands extending 62.5 miles (a hundred kilometers) in either direction of the border. This would include San Diego and Las Cruces, New Mexico, but exclude such other cities as San Antonio, Tucson, and Monterrey in Mexico that share elements of the border society and economy. For purposes of discussing environmental issues, both the U.S. and Mexican governments use the hundred-kilometer definition of the borderlands as established by the U.S.-Mexican Transboundary Environmental Cooperation Treaty (commonly known as the La Paz Treaty) in 1983.

With population or culture used as a guideline, the borderlands could be said to extend much farther north into the United States. After all, there are more people of Mexican descent living in San Francisco than in Nogales, Arizona. Waxing philosophical, some say the border is pushing its way into the Midwest, the Southeast, or wherever immigrants from Latin America are found. In the context of regional economic integration, there is much pondering about the fading of borders, and *American Demographics* magazine even heralds a new "hypernation" emerging out of the North American nations. Similar speculation revolves around an ever-expanding "third nation," which some call MexAmerica, being shaped around the cultural and social integration of Mexico's *el norte* and the U.S. Southwest.

No clear consensus exists as to where the borderlands begin and end. For different purposes, a broader or more strict spacial definition of the borderlands may be more fitting. But as border scholar Jorge Bustamante has observed, two fundamental concepts are crucial in defining the borderlands. One is a recognition of internationality as a definitive characteristic of border life, and the second is that border societies and economies are continually interactive.[11]

Chapter 1

Life on the Line

International social and economic crisscrossing does make the borderlands special. In some U.S. border towns, Spanish is more common than English. Cross-border baseball teams, marathons, and Lions Clubs are common, especially in smaller border towns. At one point the mayors of both Columbus, New Mexico, and Palomas, Chihuahua, had wives from the other side of the line. Retail trade and tourism tightly link border economies, and city planners and border scholars are beginning to talk of transfrontier metropolises that cross the international border. Los Dos Laredos and Ambos Nogales have long existed in the parlance of those border towns. In recent years, as cross-border awareness increases, the kind of informal microdiplomacy that has characterized relations between twin cities has expanded to include more formal agreements that facilitate cooperative problem solving.

Historically, formal cross-border cooperation has occurred mostly on a federal level. The prototype of a transboundary organization is the International Boundary and Water Commission (IBWC), which has counterpart organizational structures on both sides. Although eminently successful in carrying out its main mission—maintaining a trouble-free international demarcation—the binational commission does not have the mandate to address the multitude of environmental, infrastructure, development, and public health problems that now plague the border. In fact, its overly technical view of the border (seeing the Rio Grande first as an international boundary and only secondarily as a river or ecological system, for instance) obscures the larger problems that confront this heavily urbanized and industrialized region.[12]

City governments and agencies have begun to work together formally to solve specific problems and to begin to address their joint status as twin cities. San Diego and Tijuana are leading the way in this regard, having established regular communications between police departments and even hosting joint city council meetings. The binational health councils along the border also illustrate the benefits of transboundary cooperation. Rather than risk violating international protocol the border towns sometimes have found that informal channels work best, each side helping the other when special needs arise.

Highlighting the special character of the borderlands, a report by a commission created by the U.S. Congress to study international migration observed: "A unique culture has developed there, one quite distrustful of initiatives coming from either Washington or Mexico City. Mexican and U.S. border cities are economically interdependent. Hundreds of millions of legal border crossings take place each year—for shopping, work, entertainment, or medical treatment—creating an amalgam of U.S. and Mexican society."[13]

The economic interdependence and social integration of the borderlands can be overemphasized. Although the judges and city officials in Laredo speak Spanish, few on the U.S. side of the border would trade in their U.S. citizenship for a Mexican passport. San Diego promotes itself as "America's Finest City," while Tijuana advertises that it is the "Most Visited City." More evident than the integrated character of the twin cities is the fact that they belong to two different worlds and realities: One side is the edge of the developed world, the industrialized North, while the cities on the other side are the outposts of the underdeveloped South.

Borderlands unity is also undermined by east-west differences. On both sides of the international line, the borderlands are highly segmented. Historically, the predominant social and economic interactions have been in a north-south direction. This north-south dynamic is accentuated by the lack of an east-west transportation network, particularly in Mexico where it seems that all roads, rail lines, and air routes head north-sorth and there are few east-west links. Although most of the region's residents nearby identify themselves as borderlanders, these is a lack of homogeneity and social cohesion. This is particularly evident on the U.S. side because of the differences among the white, Mexican-American, and native Mexican population groups.[14]

Ambiguity pervades border life. Economically the border barely exists, but the border is real enough when it comes to labor mobility, customs and immigration checks, and as a dividing line between two markedly different systems of social and political organization. Even though the Mexican twins are generally much larger and even more industrialized than the U.S. border towns, the greater wealth, social organization, and power of the United States are readily evident.

On one side, most of the streets are paved; on the other side, most are rutted and dusty. On the one side, the tap water is drinkable; on the other one doesn't dare. On one side of the line, there are adequate sewage and drainage systems, but on the other side, one does not flush paper down the toilet, and raw sewage drains through open canals. Looking over from the dusty *colonias* of Juárez toward the shimmering banks and office buildings of downtown El Paso shatters any wild notions about a third transboundary nation being born. A tortilla in the north or a Pizza Hut in the south does not necessarily mean that the two sides are merging.

This tension between unity and division is evident in the cultural mix of the borderlands. Mexican food and the Spanish language are part of the character of the U.S. Southwest. On the Mexican side, many prefer hamburgers to burritos, and English words have been incorporated into border slang. For the most part, this cultural interpenetration is not a matter of conquest or reconquest but an internationalization process common to all international borders. Mexican officials and intellectuals in the country's interior have long criticized the *anglicismos*, like *puchear* (to push) or *la troca* (truck), that pepper the language of *fronterizos*, complaining that *el norte* was letting its cultural heritage slip away. Certainly English-language music, movies, and advertising are common throughout the northern borderlands, but not as common as in the elite circles of Mexico City. As in most cross-border interactions there is a marked asymmetry that arises from the economic imbalance between the two nations. Not only are Mexicans consuming more hamburgers but they are eating them at McDonald's and Burger King. Fueled by a larger consuming public and powered by a flood of advertising, the U.S. business/cultural complex is gradually eating away at Mexico's cultural core.

In an epoch of globalization and international communications, too much can be made of cultural imperialism. But identity is important. Is a new international borderlands identity being shaped, or is Mexico's border region just another colony falling into the grasp of U.S. shopping-mall and fast-food imperialism? It is true that the cultural landscape of Mexican border towns has long been influenced by the United States. But the economic liberalization policies of the Mexican government combined with the forces of globalization have accelerated this process.[15]

Borderlands Development

Once known as the land of sunshine, silence, and adobe, the borderlands are now one of the world's most urbanized border zones.[16] International border scholar Lawrence Herzog called the U.S.-Mexico border boom the greatest demographic and economic transformation of any border zone in the world.[17] In 1900 there were fewer than a hundred thousand people living in the borderlands. Today there are at least ten million living in border *municipios* and counties, some three million more than in 1980. Virtually all the population is concentrated in the twenty-eight main twin cities, outside of which the borderlands remains a largely desolate and lonely region.[18] At current rates of growth, it is expected that the borderlands population will double in twenty-two years.[19] Virtually all of this growth is occurring in the twin cities, while nonurban areas remain largely deserted.

On the U.S. side, border growth rates have been two to three times the national average over the past four decades. The population explosion has been equally dramatic on the Mexican side, doubling the population in the northern border zone over the past two decades and rapidly converting small border towns into major metropolises.[20] Juárez and Tijuana, both estimated to have more than 1.2 million people, are among the largest cities in Mexico. About a hundred new immigrants are thought to come to live in Juárez every day, and Colonia Libertad in Tijuana is among the world's most densely inhabited urban ghettos. Sun Belt migration in the United States and northward migration in Mexico probably account for about half the population growth in the borderlands.[21]

The prospect of a regional free trade agreement has spurred new interest in the U.S.-Mexico border as a commercial and transport district. Free trade, however, is not a new concept in the borderlands. To bolster population and commercial growth, Mexico has had a long history of creating special tariff zones along its northern border, and in the mid-1980s the U.S. Congress considered a proposal to create a coproduction/free trade zone along both sides of the border. Declared or not as free trade zones, the borderlands, particularly on the Mexican side, have long benefited from free trade in the form of contraband merchandise, or *fayuca* as it is called in Mexico. In their thirst for consumer goods unavailable on their own side, border residents have long found ways to avoid all tariff and nontariff barriers to free trade. Assisting them is a thriving sector of professional smugglers.

Ever since the launching of the Border Industrialization Program, the border as a barrier dividing national economies has become more porous. The program, which took advantage of U.S. tariff provisions facilitating international production-sharing investment, opened the northern border region to U.S. export-oriented investment. Tariffs, taxes, investment controls, and other barriers to trade were waived for companies locating along the border. In 1992, more than a quarter-century later, there were some 2,100 maquiladoras employing more than 550,000 workers assembling duty-free materials into goods for export back to the United States. By the late 1980s the maquila sector—for so long treated as the exception to Mexico's protectionist economic development strategy—became the model for future export-oriented growth.

This evolution from a remote outback to a zone of mutual development has occurred in fits and starts. Although directly tied to the economic development patterns of the two nations, the explosive development of the borderlands has paralleled the history of many other international borders. As global economic integration advances, international borders that were once buffer regions far from metropolitan centers have become dynamic economic corridors. Once regarded as peripheral to mainstream society and economy, borders are now leading the way toward new models of international commerce and investment as their functions are reconceptualized.

With the transformation of global markets and financial systems, increased international migration, and the rise in production-sharing strategies, the economic barrier between the United States and Mexico has weakened.[22] The prospect of free trade will further bolster the border zone as a center for transboundary commercial exchange.

The Old Trickle-down Problem

The boom in the maquila industry, a dramatic rise in cross-border traffic, and the social and economic integration of the U.S. and Mexican borderlands have spurred economic growth. But all is not well in the borderlands, despite this surge in investment and trade. Increased economic activity has not automatically translated into prosperity for the region. On the U.S. side job growth has fallen far short of population growth, and wages remain far below national levels. Economic, environmental, and social infrastructure is manifestly inadequate, and many fear that trade liberalization will aggravate this already severe infrastructure shortfall.

Industrial development councils in U.S. border cities have been promoting the border belt since the 1950s as a low-wage region without unions and with an array of tax-breaks and subsidies for relocating companies. Promoters of U.S. border development have encouraged companies to relocate to their cities because of their proximity to Mexico but also because of the inequality of living standards on either side of the border. Companies could set up manufacturing facilities in Mexico to take advantage of the low wages while having their offices and homes of managers located on the U.S. side.

Even as some of the apparel and electronics firms that had relocated to the U.S. Sun Belt once again picked up stakes to set up maquilas on the other side, these same promotional groups have stuck to this development strategy of attracting runaway plants to the region. More recently, business and government officials have become eager for free trade even though it holds little promise for the region's low-wage and unskilled population and will surely escalate the infrastructure crisis.

Similarly, the Mexican border region has rushed into a development strategy based on maquilas and low wages with little thought given to social, environmental, and city planning. Dollars have trickled across the border and into the local economy—but not enough to pay for the social and economic infrastructure costs of development and not enough to lift the region out of poverty.

With the exception of San Diego, the U.S. borderlands is among the poorest regions in the United States. A full quarter of families there fall below the poverty line.[23] Unemployment is also higher than the U.S. average, ranging from a low of 8 percent in

San Diego to 14 percent in Brownsville. Generally, poverty levels increase from west to east, with the Texas border cities of McAllen, Laredo, and Brownsville having the highest unemployment rates in the nation in 1989 and El Paso ranking among the top ten.

In 1993 the average salary in El Paso was 72 percent of the U.S. national average. Distributing that below-average wage among the larger-than-average families of the El Paso area meant that the average per capita income was only 55 percent of the national average. El Paso economic development promoters invariably point out that El Paso/Juárez is host to more than sixty Fortune 500 companies, but this proximity has not translated into general prosperity, particularly for most of the city's population. In 1960, before the maquila program began, about 20 percent of El Paso residents had incomes below the national average. Today, that figure has swollen to 45 percent.[24]

Much of the city's population of Mexican descent is crowded into the blighted south side of the city, whereas the minority (one-third) white population inhabits the suburban subdivisions north of Interstate 10. In 1979, 29 percent of El Paso's Latino population lived below the poverty line: the figure rose to 43 percent by 1989.[25] The poverty is most evident in downtown El Paso in an area dubbed Little Chihuahua. Only a few blocks from the Westin luxury hotel and the border crossing, families crowd into small rooms in downtown tenement buildings and have no private baths.

Per capita income, low by U.S. standards, is still three to seven times higher than on the Mexican side. Even the poorest U.S. communities enjoy per capita income two to three times higher than most Mexican municipios. The economic disparity between the U.S. and Mexican sides of the border is especially striking when one realizes that the economic gap is much narrower at the border than for the two nations as a whole. Whereas the U.S. borderlands are among the poorest regions in the United States, Mexico's northern border is that country's wealthiest region.

With 16 percent of Mexico's population, the border states account for 22 percent of national income. Unemployment is minimal, although the low figures are misleading because the government counts as employed all who work at least one hour a week. Employment and wage statistics can also vary widely. In 1986, for example, 24 percent of workers in Matamoros received less than the minimum wage while only 7 percent of Tijuana workers were under the minimum.[26] Although illiteracy for the border states is about a third of that found in the other states, this does not always translate into improved employment opportunities.

As in the United States, the poorest areas are found in the eastern border states (with the prominent exception of Nuevo León) while Baja California is the state with the highest socioeconomic indicators.[27] Although the standard of living is generally much better than in the rest of Mexico, the contrast with the U.S. borderlands in most socioeconomic indicators is still staggering. While a majority of the residents of the U.S. borderlands have completed high school, only about 10 percent on the Mexican side have completed twelve years of schooling.[28] Although substantially below the national average, infant mortality in Mexico's northern zone is approximately five times that of the U.S. borderlands, where infant mortality approximates the U.S. national average.[29]

The northern border has Mexico's highest minimum wage but also the country's highest cost of living.[30] An import-dependent economy, the border region suffers more than any other part of Mexico from peso devaluations. Reductions in the peso's value constitute a boon to maquila owners, who pay their workers in the devalued pesos, but the devaluations have caused dramatic decreases in workers' spending power in this region where the cost of living is as high as 90 percent of the U.S. level.

Despite their proximity to the United States and their higher-than-average socioeconomic indicators, the Mexican border cities are not unlike most third world cities. The lack of decent and affordable housing is the most salient problem. Women and men who work all day as maids or gardeners on the U.S. side, or in modern factories owned by companies like GE and Zenith come home at night to the desperate conditions of life in the *colonias perdidas*. The land and housing shortage has pushed families onto hillsides, floodplains, and the slopes of arroyos to build their homes. At first they erect their shelters using heavy cardboard, scrap lumber, and tin sheets. Gradually they manage to construct small concrete-block homes. It takes about a day's wage to purchase a dozen cement blocks and four months' wages to buy enough materials for a basic twelve-by-twelve-foot house.[31]

The absence of proper housing is not a one-sided problem. An estimated 5,000 homeless live in El Paso and as many as fifty thousand live in nearby *colonias*. The communities referred to as *colonias* on the U.S. side are uncharted rural subdivisions of substandard housing in which families own their own plots but generally lack water, sewerage, adequate drainage, and paved roads.[32] Most *colonia* residents buy or haul their own water, but many of the *colonia* residents have septic tanks, which contaminate not only the Rio Grande and underground aquifers but also their own personal wells.

The larger Mexican border cities are infrastructure wastelands. Spreading out from the city centers, each new subdivision or squatters' settlement has assumed its own grid pattern, creating endless transportation and planning headaches. Social services fall far short of the needs of the exploding population. Every summer hundreds of dehydrated children are brought to the Juárez general hospital, which is only several minutes away from El Paso, for treatment of gastrointestinal problems resulting from severe water shortages in the *colonias*. But during the summer of 1989 the hospital's cooling and heating system was not working. Trying to find some relief from the heat, the children and other patients took to sleeping on dirty floors. In a two-month period in 1989 more than a dozen children died as a result of the intense heat and inadequate treatment for dehydration.[33] At the same time, hospital workers had to carry patients and bodies up and down the stairs because the elevators also were out of service and there was no money available to fix them.

Norteños and Fronterizos

In Mexico, *el norte* has long been a hotbed of change and influence. For that reason Mexico's leaders have regarded the northern borderlands with some apprehension. After all, the Mexican Revolution did come sweeping down from the north. A 1906 strike at the U.S.-owned Cananea copper mine in northern Sonora sparked the popular opposition against the *porfiriato* dictatorship. In 1911 the first skirmish between the *federales* and Madero's revolutionaries bloodied the frontier town of Juárez. Francisco Madero, the intellectual author of the revolution, came from the border state of Coahuila, while Pancho Villa and his followers hailed from Durango and Chihuahua. Three of the country's early postrevolutionary presidents (de la Huerta, Obregón, and Elías Calles) were Sonorans.

Although the Spanish did attempt to establish their hold on the region with frontier *presidios* or forts, they never established a strong colonial presence in the north. This rugged mountain and desert domain was the land of miners and ranchers. No major prehispanic civilization arose from the north, and the native peoples that did make a home here (the Yaquis in the Pacific lowlands and the Tarahumaras in the Sierra Madre) had few relations with the *norteños*. From the beginning it was a land of tough and self-reliant Mexicans who tended to think and act more independently than those from the interior.[34]

Not only have they been more affected by the modernizing winds of the north, but these people have also had a long history of contact with U.S. companies—the railroads, mines, and agri-businesses. It was no coincidence that Monterrey, Mexico's industrial center, rose in the north, only 140 miles from the border.

Since the mid-1800s the Mexican government has been seeking ways to keep its remote northern border tied to the country's center. During the Cárdenas administration (1934-40) the government sought to develop and populate the northern border with irrigation and land-distribution programs. Worried that the *fronterizos* were losing their language and culture, the government sponsored special educational and civic programs to keep the language pure and patriotism strong.

In the early 1980s there seemed to be a new revolution stirring in the north as the National Action Party (PAN) began building a strong anti-PRI (Institutional Revolutionary Party) movement there. It was both a civic rebellion against the PRI dictatorship and a declaration that the time had come for the private sector to be put in the driver's seat. The PRI's wholehearted embrace of free-market economic policies took some of the wind out of PAN's sails, but widespread public disgust with the PRI bureaucracy has kept PAN strong.

Improved communication and transportation links as well as its own economic strength mean that the region is no longer so isolated from the centers of power in Mexico. Today the *fronterizos* and *norteños* are increasingly following U.S. economic and political models. The people here look not to Mexico City but to the north for their styles, culture, and ideology. *Norteño* ballads and *rancheras* are still popular in the *cantinas*, but *fronterizos* are also rooting for the Dallas Cowboys and Los Angeles Dodgers. Along the border the demand for U.S. goods is evident, but for most they are not affordable. Advertising, proximity to the United States, and the increasing presence of U.S. retail outlets in Mexico are importing U.S. consumer habits to a people who cannot afford U.S. consumer goods.

The northern borderlands have also become the destination for used vehicles, clothes, tires, appliances, and just about everything else discarded by the United States. Downtown stores in U.S. border cities advertise *Ropa americana por libra* (American clothes by the pound). A baled bundle of used clothes cost $5.98 at one El Paso outlet. "We're becoming a secondhand society living off the waste of the U.S.," lamented Victor Clark Alfaro, a human rights activist in Tijuana.[35]

At the border, U.S. visitors enter Mexico to seek the old—street vendors, posed photographs in donkey carts, and handicrafts from Old Mexico. Heading north—legally or illegally—are those who seek the new. They want part of the future and think they will be able to find it only across this magical line. As Carlos Monsiváis wrote: "The heart of the Mexican dream is Los Angeles."[36] It is the land where dreams wait to be realized.

The Latinization of the United States

You do not have to be a demographer to know that the ethnic and cultural composition of U.S. society is rapidly changing. The predominance of an English-speaking population of European descent persists, but this majority is diminishing in the face of the more rapidly expanding population of immigrants and ethnic minorities. Bilingual signs in airports and government buildings, Spanish-language billboards and media, and the emergence of strong but insular Guatemalan, Cuban, Vietnamese, South Korean, Salvadoran, and Mexican communities in U.S. cities are among the most obvious signs of this demographic change. The rise of "English Only" campaigns and immigration-control movements, boosted by widespread fears of a declining U.S. economy, are signs of a reaction to this population shift that is redefining U.S. society.

Most prominent, especially in the U.S. Southwest, has been the rise of that part of the U.S. population labeled Hispanic by the U.S. Census Bureau but increasingly referred to as Latinos by community leaders. In 1950, 2.6 percent of the U.S. population was Hispanic, it rose to 4.7 percent by 1970 and 9 percent by 1990.[37] Hispanics are increasing in number about five times faster than Anglos and are expected to constitute about 13 percent of the U.S. population by the year 2010.[38]

Between 1980 and 1990 the Latino population in California increased from 19 percent of the state to 26 percent. Most dramatic was the increase in Los Angeles, where the number of Latino residents in the county rose 62 percent in the 1980s. If this trend continues, more Latinos than Anglos will reside in Los Angeles by 2010.[39] Buoyed by such statistics, State Senator Art Torres proclaimed: "The legacy of Los Angeles left by its founding fathers and mothers—Spanish, Indian, and Mexican—is now being reclaimed by a new generation of leaders."[40] Indeed, the population statistics are auspicious for Latino politicians hoping to capture the new Latino vote and to put forward a Latino political agenda.[41]

Immigration is a major factor in the Latino population growth, with the U.S. Census Bureau estimating in 1990 that more than 40 percent of Latinos, or more than nine million current residents, were born outside the United States. About half of California's Latino growth in the past decade came from legal and undocumented immigration.[42] Because immigrants tend to be young and Latino families large, the Latino population is much younger than the U.S. average—a median age of 25.3 years compared with 33.6 years for the balance of the U.S. population. Just 5 percent of Latinos in the United States are over age sixty five compared with more than 13 percent for non-Latinos. Immigrants compose only about 7 percent of the U.S. labor force but have accounted for 22 percent of the growth in the work force since 1970 and are expected to constitute 25 percent of that growth in the 1990s.[43]

Immigrant Latinos may share a Latin American birthplace (Mexico, Central America, South America, and the Spanish-speaking Caribbean—Puerto Rico, Cuba, and the Dominican Republic) and the Spanish language, but they do not fit collectively into one social sector. Their cultures, lifestyles, class backgrounds, race, language cadences and accents, and political inclinations differ sharply. The cultural mix within the United States can be truly grasped only through an understanding of what each of the twenty nationalities brings to this society.

In the effort to establish a common political agenda and in recognition of some social commonalities (such as being Spanish speaking and having familial origins in Latin America), many politicians and academics have favored the use of such generic terms as *Hispanic* and *Latino*. In recent years, the term Latino has gained increased acceptance, especially in political and academic circles. Many frown on the use of Hispanic, charging that those who prefer that label are trying to whiten or Europeanize their identities by accenting their Spanish rather than Latin American, *mestizo*, or African heritage.

The term Latino is regarded as more race neutral and more reflective of Latin American origins. Although useful for political, marketing, and census purposes, the Hispanic and Latino labels disguise the many racial, national-origin, and class differences among the different communities.[44] Such pan-ethnic terms also fail to distinguish between the native and foreign born.[45]

In the 1990 U.S. census, Mexican origin became a subcategory of Spanish or Hispanic origin. Mexican-origin residents represented 2 percent of the population in 1970, rising to 5 percent by 1990. Census figures show that 80 percent of Hispanic-origin Californians were of Mexican descent, and 91 percent of Hispanic-origin Texans were of Mexican descent.[46] Two border states, California and Texas, were homes to 54 percent of Latinos, followed by New York, Florida, Illinois, New Jersey, Arizona, New Mexico, and Colorado.[47]

Mexicans and Mexican Americans are the largest population group in most border towns—San Diego being the usual exception to border generalizations, with the Latino share being just 20 percent. The largest majorities are found along the Texas border, ranging from 69 percent in El Paso to 97 percent in Starr County. Persons of Mexican origin are the fastest-growing minority in the United States and are projected to be the "majority minority" in California by the year 2030.[48] In 1990 U.S. residents of Mexican-origin constituted 64 percent of all Latinos in the United States.

Except for the self-labeled Hispanos of northern New Mexico (whose ancestors lived in the area long before Mexico declared its independence from Spain), well over 90 percent of the Latinos of the borderlands could be aptly termed Mexican Americans, meaning Americans of Mexican descent. However, because of the negative stereotyping by the Anglos of the region, it was not until the late 1950s that the term Mexican American became an accepted self-designation.

Especially in the nineteenth century the term Mexican—or "Mess-can" as it was commonly pronounced—connoted halfbreed, intellectually inferior, indolent, dishonest, backward, and treacherous.[49] By calling themselves Spanish, Mexican Americans established some distance between themselves and their Mexican roots. They sought to avoid the negative stereotyping while at the same time benefiting from the European or white connotation of Spanish ancestry.[50]

In the late 1950s and especially in the 1960s the term Mexican American came into widespread use with the founding of the Mexican American Political Association, United Mexican American Students, and other groups who wanted to affirm their Mexican ancestry. Other Mexican-origin Latinos, especially university students and militant community organizers, adopted the term Chicano—a derivative of *mexicano*—in the spirit of the new nationalism that was building throughout the Southwest and the nation, whose models in many ways were the civil rights and black-power movements.[51] In fact, the increasingly common use of Chicano eased the acceptance of Mexican American as a self-identifier.[52]

Closely associated with the brown-power nationalist sentiment of the early Chicano movement was a conception that the *mestizos* of the Southwest together with the Mexican people formed part of the mythical nation of Aztlán.[53] They were all part of the "Cosmic Race," the utopian term first used in 1920 by Mexican intellectual José Vasconcelos in a reference to a "fifth race" or a *raza de bronce* (bronze race) that melds other races together.[54] Colloquially they were la raza—a term meaning "our people." The cultural nationalism of the early Chicano leaders was clearly expressed in the Plan de Santa Barbara, the manifesto of the 1960s Chicano movement, which asserted there was a "crucial distinction in political consciousness between a Mexican American and a Chicano mentality. The Mexican American is a person who lacks respect for his cultural and ethnic heritage . . . . In contrast, Chicanismo reflects self-respect and pride in one's own heritage and cultural background." Gradually the less restrictive definition of a Chicano as a person of Mexican ancestry but not an immigrant gained acceptance throughout the Southwest but particularly among students, militants, politicians, and progressives.

Along with the cultural nationalism of the 1960s there arose many illusions about how culturally pure and politically correct Mexico was. This idealism was soon shattered as romantic notions of Mexico clashed with the reality of the widespread oppression, racism, and exploitation that exist in Mexico. For many Chicanos, the green, white, and red colors of the Mexican flag—once appropriated as their own cultural banner—faded as a symbol of their own ethnic pride because of their rising confusion and disillusionment about Mexico.

The struggle over terminology reflects the long-running identification crisis faced by Mexican Americans. Racism and negative stereotyping lie at the heart of this cultural crisis, but the search for self-identity has also been complicated by the conflicting attitudes about Mexico, assimilationist ambitions, internalized repression, and the economic and political marginalization of the Mexican American people.

The positioning of Mexican Americans with regard to Mexico and Mexican immigrants has long been a source of tension and conflict. This has been seen most clearly in the debate over immigration laws. Although there exists broad sympathy for immigrants, Latino concern that immigration threatens hard-won social and economic progress is also widespread. In recessionary times, anti-immigrant sentiment tends to rise.

The stagnant U.S. economy in recent years has stalled the economic progress of Latinos. In 1990, 23 percent of all Latino families and 20 percent of all Mexican-origin families existed below the poverty line—compared with 9 percent for all U.S. families.[55] According to a 1990 report on the status of U.S. Latinos, two-thirds of all Latinos "lack the skills required for stable employment that pays a reasonable wage." Furthermore, the study found that 40 percent of those age twenty-five to thirty-four had not completed four years of high school, and that the real median income of Latinos had fallen between 1979 and 1987 in all but four of the thirteen metropolitan areas surveyed.[56]

But one must be careful in making cultural, social, and economic characterizations based on generic labels. Generalized descriptions of the socioeconomic status of Latinos point to the inexactitude of such umbrella terms as Latino or Hispanic. This standardized terminology also leads to racial and cultural stereotyping when in fact there exist major socioeconomic differences within the various U.S. minority (mainly Mexican Americans and Puerto Ricans) and immigrant groups (Cubans, Dominicans, Central Americans, Mexicans, and South Americans) of Latin American descent. Most obvious is the privileged economic status of the middle-and upper-class Cuban-American community. But sharp class distinctions also exist within the various ethnic groupings, and the large influx of poor immigrants from Mexico and Central America tends to obscure the socioeconomic advances being made by the native-born Latinos.

Although it is often argued that free trade would boost economic growth in the Southwest, virtually all the studies of NAFTA's probable impact have concluded that the sector of the population likely to be most adversely affected and displaced are low-skilled, low-wage workers—a sector in which Latino workers are disproportionately represented.[57] Latino organizations such as National Council of La Raza and Mexican American Legal Defense and Education Fund (MALDEF) provided strong initial support for NAFTA, including backing "fast track" negotiations. But in response to rising concerns about trade liberalization with Mexico and other less developed countries, some Latino organizations later took a more even-handed although still largely supportive positions with respect to the proposed free trade agreement. According to Antonio González, a project director for Southwest Voter Research Institute, "The predominant tendency among Latinos is 'compassion for Mexico but don't take my job.' "[58]

For Latinos, political power is not necessarily proportionate to their numbers. Dramatic increases in the number of Latino public officials, especially at the state and local levels, do indicate that the tables are turning. But voter registration and turnouts far below national averages continue to frustrate Latino politicians. Hispanic turnout in the 1992 elections was 29 percent, compared to 54 percent for Blacks. Voter registration rates for Hispanics have not improved over the past two decades. In fact, there has been a decline in the percentage of Hispanics that are registered, dropping from 44 percent and 38 percent in 1972 and 1976 respectively, to 35 percent in both the 1988 and 1992 elections.

The low registration and turnout rates for Latinos are partly explained by the large noncitizen population. Omitting noncitizens from the population base would raise Latino turnout in 1992 to 48 percent.[59] Another factor explaining low voter participation is the higher percentage of Latinos who are in their late teens and early twenties—a group that shows low participation rates in most ethnic categories. Language barriers and the traditional marginalization of Latino communities also help explain low voter participation. However, the fact that voter registration has held steady since 1988 indicates that efforts by groups such as the Southwest Voter Education Project have prevented further decline despite the rapid increase in the number of eligible Latino voters.

A monolithic Latino voting bloc can not be assumed by Latino politicians.[60] Latino support for Democratic candidates is likely but can no longer be counted on. Not only are Latino voters increasingly split between Democratic, Republican, and independents, but they are also divided by their diverse countries of origin, cultures, class backgrounds, and divergent aspirations.[61] Shaping a common political agenda for Latinos has proved difficult not only because the various communities of Latin American descent do not share a common sense of identity but because of diverse political views and class status both within and between the different ethnic groups. This is especially true on foreign policy issues but also extends to such domestic issues as affirmative action, immigration reform, and abortion.[62] Among most groups there does, however, exist a strong support for bilingual education and for increased government services.[63]

Conservative immigration-reform groups, some environmental organizations, and population control groups all raise concerns about the effect of "Latinization" on the quality of life in the United States. They suggest that the large immigrant population, legal and illegal, is contributing to social fragmentation while taking jobs from native-born citizens and overtaxing the country's social services.[64] Furthermore, the unprecedented stream of Latino immigrants in recent decades has given rise to large ethnic populations of Mexicans, Salvadorans, and Guatemalans that do not speak English, do not participate in the U.S. political process, and do not make it through the educational system. Although gradually assimilating, their social isolation and lack of personal resources together with racial barriers hinder this process.

Others celebrate the immigrant presence, pointing out that the United States has long been a nation of immigrants and arguing that immigrants are good for the U.S. economy. Moreover, the percentage of U.S. residents who are foreign born—about 6 percent—is far below the 14 percent of the high point of immigration in the 1900-1920 period. Not only are today's immigrants generally younger than the average population but they tend not to use social services (except for education) as much as native-born citizens.[65] Immigration proponents also argue that immigrant workers make the U.S. economy more competitive, have only a slight impact on wage levels, and do not cause massive job displacement.[66]

Mexican immigration—and by extension all south-north immigration into the United States—is a national and international phenomenon that goes to the heart of U.S.-Mexican relations. It involves, as we will examine in the next chapter, such larger questions as the economic imbalances between nations, the failure of economic development models in third world countries, and the impact of free trade and globalization of production on international labor mobility. Especially for borderlands communities, these are more than abstract questions—they are features of everyday life.

Chapter 2

Crossover Dreams—and Nightmares

On an average day, between 7,000 and 9,000 people enter the United States illegally over its border with Mexico. The crossings are surprisingly visible. Standing on the Paso del Norte bridge in El Paso, one can watch passengers unload from cars in Juárez in broad daylight, walk down the southern bank of the Rio Grande, cross over either by foot or on rafts run by entrepreneurs, climb up the northern bank, pay a small entrance fee to thugs or scouts, and enter the United States through holes in the cyclone fence. In and near San Diego, where nearly half the crossings occur, hundreds of people gather at nightfall in a few areas. Along the few lighted stretches of the border, or with the help of night vision equipment, one can view their subsequent dash through the fence and over the scrub brush. At times television news viewers have seen terrifying footage of large groups of immigrants sprinting north through San Diego's southbound border crossing, directly into oncoming freeway traffic.

Images such as these have contributed to a feeling among many Americans that the country has lost control of its borders. Headlines describing "floods" or "tidal waves" of illegal immigrants, political rhetoric about a "silent invasion," and greatly exaggerated estimates of the numbers of undocumented foreigners have had a similar effect. Perceptions that they take jobs from legal U.S. residents or at least undercut wages and working conditions add to the resentment of undocumented immigrants. Throughout the United States there is also widespread concern that they burden the social welfare and education systems and that some cross into the United States to commit crimes, returning to Mexico to escape capture.[67] These concerns are particularly prevalent in the U.S. borderlands, where local governments feel that the federal government has left border communities without the financial resources to address the problems created by increased legal and illegal immigration. According to Augie Bareño, director of San Diego's Department of Transborder Affairs, recent U.S. immigration laws that have granted widespread amnesty and increased legal immigration "have influenced the politics and public opinion of the United States and particularly of the border region. This has created, unintentionally, a very severe, very profound, and very mean anti-immigrant spirit."[68]

These issues are not new.[69] They have been the subject of popular debate since the 1920s, when Mexican migration first became an important national issue in this country. The negative perceptions of illegal immigration have exerted considerable pressure for action on legislators—especially those from border states. Historically, this pressure has produced periodic deportation campaigns—generally corresponding to U.S. economic downturns—and a variety of immigration reforms.[70] But none of these efforts has put a stop to illegal immigration, and their deterrent effect has generally been short-term. The United States has proved unable to design or unwilling to enforce policies that would "seal the borders," as some have hoped.

Criminals or International Workers?

Near the fetid green water of the Tijuana River, a graffiti artist has tagged the south side of the wall with a message: "Neither illegals nor criminals—international workers." The sentiment of the message is accurate even if undocumented immigrants do commit the misdemeanor of "entry without inspection." By far the majority of Mexican immigrants are workers who cross the boundary in search of decent jobs or family members of those workers. These international workers have made significant contributions to the development of the United States and the profitability of U.S. business.

The demand for labor by U.S. railroad companies and later by agribusinesses began to pull Mexican workers into the western United States in the 1880s. Expanding rapidly into the southwest, the Southern Pacific and Santa Fe railroads developed a rapacious appetite for cheap labor. Realizing that Mexicans would be much more convenient than the then-favored Chinese coolies, the railroad companies began recruiting from the south. Mexicans lived much closer than the Chinese, were almost as desperate, and could easily be sent home when no longer needed.

By 1910 approximately twenty thousand Mexicans were being recruited each year by agents for the railroad companies. Other industries also began recruiting in Mexico or illegally paying labor contractors and smugglers to bring workers across the border. Mexican labor formed the backbone of the westward spread of cotton plantations and for the proliferation of large-scale vegetable, fruit, and sugar beet plantations. To a lesser extent, Mexican workers contributed to the development of copper mining in the Southwest.[71] During World War I, when native-born labor was in especially short supply, Mexicans played a critical role in sustaining the U.S. economy.

When World War I ended, however, the United States expressed little gratitude for the contributions of Mexican labor. Deep schisms began to develop within U.S. society around the issue of Mexican immigration. Businesses fought to defend their access to the cheap and abundant Mexican labor supply. Opposing them were labor unions and a growing anti-immigrant sentiment among the general public. This division set the stage for seventy years of policy debate and international conflict.

The return of the doughboys and the postwar recession of 1921-22 made Mexicans outcasts, especially among workers threatened with or suffering from unemployment. With the encouragement of labor leaders and some politicians, mobs attacked Mexicans at work, at home, and in the streets. But at the same time, U.S. employers—particularly growers, railroads, and the auto and steel industries—continued to recruit Mexicans. Their agents sought cheap labor both in Mexico itself and in the vast Mexican labor pool that had accumulated in Texas. The Mexican workers they hired lived in fear of deportation because of the heightened anti-immigrant atmosphere.

Unable to seek justice from the authorities, workers were unlikely to complain about common abuses, ranging from unsafe working conditions and underpayment of wages to beatings and robberies. As continued to be true in the coming decades, efforts to rid the country of undocumented residents did not prevent employers from hiring them. Instead, anti-immigrant measures actually increased the benefits to employers of hiring undocumented workers by increasing workers' vulnerability to abuse.[72]

The Great Depression dealt an even harsher blow to Mexican immigrant workers. Hundreds of thousands were rounded up and deported. Unemployment in manufacturing and mining eliminated those jobs, and by the late 1930s the Dust Bowl migration to California meant that growers there no longer needed Mexicans to perform stoop labor.

Mexican migration entered a new cycle with the onset of World War II. Again the country faced a labor shortage, and U.S. recruiters were back in Mexico looking for temporary farm workers. Washington assisted the recruitment effort by negotiating an executive agreement with Mexico in 1942 called the Emergency Farm Labor Program. Under the *bracero* program, as it became known, the U.S. government hired Mexicans chosen by the Mexican government and then subcontracted the workers out to growers. The U.S. government guaranteed transportation and the payment of a minimum wage. The *bracero* program continued in a variety of forms until 1964.[73] In the late 1950s, more than four hundred thousand *braceros* worked legally each year on U.S. farms and orchards.

The Mexican government had serious misgivings about sending its citizens abroad and about the vulnerability of *braceros* to abuse by their employers. But the money the workers sent back was so valuable to the Mexican economy that the country never decided to halt the program. In the end the U.S. government called it off. In part this was due to the growing civil rights and farmworker-organizing movements, which increased the nation's concern over the living and working conditions of immigrant workers. The program's cancellation was also due to decreased demand for legal *braceros* that stemmed from mechanical innovations such as the tomato harvester, introduced in the early 1960s.

The *bracero* program failed to halt undocumented immigration from Mexico to the United States. Many more illegal immigrants crossed the border from 1942 to 1964 than did legally contracted *braceros*, the large majority to work in seasonal agriculture. But when the program was combined with an enforcement campaign launched in 1954 called Operation Wetback, there was a large drop in the number of Mexicans apprehended crossing the border illegally. In 1953 the Immigration and Naturalization Service (INS) apprehended nearly 900,000 undocumented foreigners; this figure dropped to 250,000 in 1955 and to 88,000 in 1956. Upon the termination of the *bracero* program, illegal immigration accelerated rapidly. In 1976 INS apprehensions passed one million.[74]

From the railroads to modern agribusiness, U.S. employers and Mexican workers established a seasonal migratory pattern that continued for decades. Few immigrants crossed with the intention of staying in the United States. Migrant workers usually came from small, often isolated towns and villages concentrated heavily in the poor agricultural states of central Mexico. Earning enough to support their families was the nearly universal motive behind migration.

Dramatic changes in the Mexican economy during the 1980s produced a shift in the nature of migration. Drastic cuts in government services, huge outflows of capital, and the loss of export markets meant soaring unemployment and an end to most government support for small farmers. Within Mexico millions of people migrated from the countryside to large cities no longer able to eke out a living from barely arable land. Hundreds of thousands migrated to Mexico's northern border, seeking employment in the burgeoning maquiladora assembly plants. In the cities, millions were forced into the informal economy, as street vendors, window washers, and beggars. The call of the north became more persuasive than ever. Increasingly, migrants came from and headed to large urban centers, rather than to farming communities. These migrants were looking for jobs in the service sector—with restaurants, hotels, car washes, and construction firms—or in manufacturing. Although some of them were coming only temporarily, more appeared to have given up hope of ever earning a living in Mexico and came planning to stay.[75]

The overall economic effect on Mexico of the migration of its citizens to the United States is unclear. On the one hand, Mexican nationals in the United States—with and without documents—send huge sums of money to their families relative to what they could earn in Mexico. This is extremely important for the Mexican economy, possibly surpassing the country's income from either tourism, the maquiladora program, or foreign direct investment. A 1992 study placed the amount between $2 billion and $6.2 billion for 1990, and strongly suggested that the actual amount was closer to the upper limit than the lower.[76]

On the other hand, the exodus of people represents a loss of human capital, and because immigration requires planning and fortitude, emigrants tend to be the ambitious, entrepreneurial individuals that the Mexican government is counting on to revitalize the country's economy as the state's role shrinks. Many studies indicate that the money sent to Mexico by workers in the United States does not contribute to long-term economic development. Instead it goes to the purchase of consumer goods, many of which are imported.[77]

Like It or Not, Here We Come

The swath of land where the United States meets Mexico is both the place where the interdependence and integration of the two countries are most apparent and the scene of the most determined efforts to keep a strict dividing line between them. Deployment of military troops, the use of high-tech detection systems, and the imposition of forbidding physical barriers at the border have undoubtedly succeeded in turning back some of the immigrant stream. But they fall far short of being long-term solutions.

Perhaps nobody knows this better than the Border Patrol agents themselves. Every day they get a dose of global economic and political reality: peasants with no productive land and no hope of getting any, workers with no decent jobs and no hope of getting them, Central Americans frightened and tired of living under repressive governments, and Mexicans who simply want a better life for their families and children. Put in the position of the "aliens" they chase, these custodians of the border would probably make the same choice to take the long trip north.

For the most part, it comes down to economics. No matter how frustrating or unrewarding, many Border Patrol keep their jobs because the pay is good. The United States may be in a state of economic decline and the standard of living is slipping, but it still looks like the land of opportunity to millions living outside its borders. Immigration scholars have long discussed the "push" and "pull" factors contributing to international migrant streams. Generally these refer to the conditions of poverty and political repression that push people out of their own homes and the higher wages and increased opportunities that pull them toward another country.

The poorest of the poor are not the main immigrants. Rather, immigrants tend to be community members who are better off than their neighbors and have the savings to afford the necessary bus tickets, bribes, and coyotes (immigrant smugglers). They are also the "risk takers" of their communities in their willingness to chance failure and unknown hardships. Clearly, the closer one is to the United States, the less expensive and less arduous the migration. That explains, at least partially, why Mexico has historically lost more of its citizens to the United States than have more distant Latin American countries.

But the economics of immigration are not that simple. Domestic factors such as overpopulation, increasing poverty, and political repression are not the only forces pushing international migration flows. Saskia Sassen, an expert on global restructuring at Columbia University, has concluded that capital mobility and foreign intervention also fuel labor mobility. When the political and economic systems of nations become interconnected, labor tends to flow to the country where there is less social stratification and higher standards of living.[78] Just as the advance of European capitalism and technology resulted in migration to Europe from the affected African and Asian countries, so too has the U.S. global reach set off migratory flows from countries like the Philippines, Vietnam, South Korea, the Dominican Republic, Haiti, El Salvador, Nicaragua, and Mexico.

Economic expansionism (foreign trade, investment, and financial dealings) together with an interventionist foreign policy helps establish the context for international migration. According to Sassen, "The central role played by the United States in the emergence of a global economy over the past 30 years lies at the core of why people migrate here in ever-increasing numbers. U.S. efforts to open its own and other countries' economies to the flow of capital, goods, services, and information created conditions that mobilized people for migration, and formed linkages between the United States and other countries that subsequently served as bridges for migration."[79]

One of the earliest and clearest examples of economic integration that sparked migration to the United States was seen in Puerto Rico, where U.S. investment in export-oriented manufacturing and U.S.-led agricultural modernization established the international context for migration. Peasants who found they no longer had a vital place in the domestic economy because of U.S. investment in sugar plantations or nontraditional agroexports saw the folly of working at home for third world wages when they might be able to find the same kind of job in the United States for much higher ones. In the case of Mexico, the *bracero* program established a strong link between Mexican labor and U.S. capital, forming a migratory pattern that to a certain extent still exists in U.S. agriculture. Likewise the maquila program did create jobs, but it also caused many Mexicans from the interior to look north for opportunity.

Economic growth does not necessarily slow out-migration. Although their own economies were booming, many Taiwanese and South Koreans chose to leave for the United States, which they judged would offer more possibilities for upward mobility. Uneven development, often a product of modernizing economic growth, also results in international migration. As Sassen has observed, "Measures commonly thought to deter emigration—foreign investment, or the promotion of export-oriented agriculture and manufacturing in poor countries—have had precisely the opposite effect. Such investment contributes to massive displacement of small-scale agricultural and manufacturing enterprises, while simultaneously deepening the economic, cultural, and ideological ties between recipient countries and the United States."[80] These factors all encourage migration—something to consider when evaluating claims that U.S.-Mexico free trade will slow the tide of migration from Mexico.

Global economic restructuring and integration have clearly raised the levels of international migration, but these same economic forces are also changing the labor market in the United States. At a time when traditional highly paid manufacturing jobs have become scarce, new immigrants are finding a place in the expanding informal and low-skilled services economy. Moreover, the post-World War II collaboration of capital and labor is breaking down as U.S. companies become transnational and U.S. workers have been increasingly forced to compete with foreign workers employed by U.S.-owned firms.[81] As union shops disappear, low-wage jobs in nonunion workplaces expand. Technological development has created a narrow sector of highly paid technicians, consultants, and information specialists. But they depend on armies of poorly paid women and men working dead-end jobs assembling parts, pushing paper, entering data, and cleaning office buildings.

The restructuring of capital-labor relations has resulted in increased economic polarization, with those at the top experiencing the "need" for more personal services—dog walkers, errand runners, restaurant workers, and gardeners—to maintain their lifestyles. Hard-working immigrants struggling for economic footholds often fill these slots. The restructuring of the U.S. family has contributed to this demand. With the rise of the two-income family, U.S. workers do not have time for household work tradition-ally performed by housewives; childcare becomes a necessity when both parents are working, and in many areas there is a ready supply of Mexican women willing to take children into their own homes for as little as one dollar an hour. No longer are maids, nannies, and other household help the exclusive province of the very wealthy. Pro-fessional couples are finding that they too can join the garden econ-omy by paying (in cash with no taxes) Mexican immigrants to do their shopping, gardening, and cleaning. Also forming part of this expanding informal ("off-the-books") economy of immigrant labor are skilled workers who do dry-walling, electricity, car repair, sewing, and construction work for low fees.

Many immigration experts and economists argue that the entry of recent immigrants into the manufacturing sector, especially small-batch producers with flexible production strategies, is help-ing keep the U.S. economy competitive.[82] Agribusiness, although increasingly mechanized, remains heavily dependent on immi-grant and other Latino labor. Seventy percent of migrant farm-workers are Mexican men, and only 3 percent of migrants are non-Latino U.S.-born workers.[83]

A strong argument can also be made that the aging U.S. soci-ety needs the injection of primarily young immigrants. During the 1990s the number of U.S. citizens age eighty-five and older is projected by the Census Bureau to grow by 42 percent—about six times the rate of overall population growth. At a time when the U.S. work force is growing older, Mexico is a young society—half the population is under the age of fifteen—and provides a contin-ual supply of young workers willing and able to do jobs unwanted by U.S. citizens. In a *Wall Street Journal* article Peter Francese, president of American Demographics, advised, "The United States needs to admit more immigrants now to get us out of the demo-graphic bind we put ourselves in by restricting immigration in the first place."[84] Immigrants, it is argued, can fill the rising need for workers to care for the elderly, the sick, children, and the handi-capped. As the slow-growing U.S. population ages, all these needs will become more acute.

Clearly the "pull" factors still exist within the U.S. economy. Despite its overall crisis, immigrant labor is still in high demand, not just by business but also by households. But labor market forces alone do not fully explain the character of the pull north. Also critical are the social factors or what immigration experts call "social networks."

To Cross Is to Die

Cruzar es morir un poco, according to a Mexican ballad. "To cross is to die a little" captures the tragedy of leaving one's home and being forced to leave one's culture, family, and even style of dress behind. For peasants, *cruzar es morir un poco* also evokes the sadness of leaving the *rancho* and the life of the *campo*.

But in its romanticism for Mother Mexico, the ballad may paint a false picture of immigration. Migration to the United States is in many communities a rite of passage for young men. Upon their return, with new clothes and a new sense of themselves, they establish themselves as eligible bachelors capable of providing for a family.

Until the 1980s most Mexican immigrants were what sociologists call sojourners, not permanent settlers. They supplied the seasonal labor needed to harvest the citrus of Arizona, the lettuce of California, and the cucumbers and chili peppers of the Lower Rio Grande Valley in Texas. Today, however, only 10 to 15 percent of the Mexicans in California, Arizona, and Texas work in seasonal agriculture. Instead they are found throughout the formal economy and constitute a major element in the booming informal economy in the United States. Increasingly Mexicans come to the United States to stay. They are settlers, and while often sad about leaving Mexico, they are hopeful about finding a new and better home in the United States.

Easing their entry into and adjustment to the new society are far-reaching social networks that make the new arrival feel at home. The most important networks are those formed by relatives and members of the same communities back home in Mexico or deeper in Latin America. Rarely does the immigrant enter the United States completely alone. Usually he or she comes with a phone number or address of some acquaintance and perhaps even instructions about how to negotiate the way there. Most head for Los Angeles or other traditional destinations, not because these are necessarily the places of most opportunity but rather because that is where their social networks lead them.

These social networks make immigration a self-perpetuating process. Each new settler in the United States becomes a magnet drawing others north. As the immigrants settle in, creating their own ties of kinship and friendship in the United States, they are no longer temporary sojourners in U.S. society but permanent residents. But each new settler creates a host of potential immigrants who dream of repeating his or her success.[85] It has also been argued, however, that the absence of social networks between the United States and some regions in Mexico makes it unlikely that there will be a surge of immigration from those regions even if economic conditions worsen.[86]

Immigrants from the south also rely on networks of social-justice activists who provide assorted services, such as immigration counseling and temporary housing, and organize on behalf of this vulnerable population. Some immigrant communities have also begun establishing their own mutual assistance networks with the help of sympathetic U.S. citizens. One such organization is the Mixtec Civic Committee, a group of Indians from the southern Mexican state of Oaxaca who work on the truck farms north of San Diego but who also have strong links with the Mixtec Indians who live and work in Baja California. Campesino Families is another mutual aid organization based in Bakersfield, California, which sponsors cooperative schools and child-care centers.

The existence of social networks established in the United States has been one reason for the changing character of the migrant stream. No longer is the stereotype of the lone Mexican campesino immigrant accurate. Entire families are coming north at the same time, and it is now common for women to cross the border alone. Over the past three decades the immigrant community has become steadily more heterogeneous, but it was Mexico's economic crisis of the early 1980s that really sparked the nontraditional immigration of urban residents and women and children. Determining that there were no prospects for economic betterment in either the *campo* or the city, they counted their savings, packed their bags, and hopped on a bus for the border.[87] As the work force in Mexico has become more integrated and as gender stereotypes slowly break down, women have decided that they, too, want a chance for a better life that crossing the line might give. Also contributing to this nontraditional immigrant stream in recent years was the 1990 immigration law that expanded the categories of family members that could qualify for legal U.S. residence. Once one family member received residency, other members also began heading north.

Fear and Loathing on the Border

Entering the United States has always been a risky proposition for the undocumented. Without legal status, they are particularly vulnerable to extortion, police brutality, economic exploitation, and racist violence. Lately the victimization of undocumented immigrants has worsened. Economic downturn in the United States, the rise of burglaries in U.S. border communities, and the increased flow of narcotics across the borderlands have all aggravated border tensions, leading to a rise in violence directed at the immigrants. Also contributing to the climate of hostility that emerged in the 1980s were alarmist warnings from the CIA, INS, and the White House about the "invasion" of our borders.[88] In 1984 President Reagan summarized this rising preoccupation with the immigrant flow from Mexico, Central America, and other Latin American nations: "The simple truth is that we've lost control of our borders, and no nation can do that and survive."[89]

Even before crossing *la linea* separating Mexico from the United States, northbound migrants must be constantly on the lookout for police and thieves. The Federal Judicial Police, *federales*, have long preyed on migrants intent on crossing to the United States. Reforms by the Salinas administration have cut down on police corruption and human rights abuses. But Mexicans, and especially Central Americans, heading to *el otro lado* still commonly find themselves victims of police corruption and violence.[90] The government's Paisano project, which is part of the nationwide Solidarity program, encourages Mexican citizens to report cases of police abuse. However, a survey in Nogales, Sonora, found that a year after the Paisano campaign was launched four out of ten migrants interviewed reported they had been victims of police misconduct.[91] When asked, most illegal immigrants say they would rather be picked up by the U.S. Border Patrol than face the brutality of the Mexican police.[92]

On their journey north the immigrants next pass through the gauntlet of thieves and rapists that haunt the border zone. In some cases, the assailants are the very men hired to guide the frightened travelers into the United States. These are the *coyotes* or *polleros* (chicken keepers) whose business is smuggling their *pollos* or human contraband into the United States. Although many are dishonest and ruthless, most are dependable and fear the *bandidos* who stalk the border as much as their clients do.

Depending on how and where the immigrants choose to cross, different risks and dangers await them. For many Mexican peasants traveling every year to the United States for seasonal farm work, the best route is the physically exhausting trip through the deserts and mountains of the Southwest. For those who know the way, there is little risk of encounters with the U.S. Border Patrol, the border enforcement arm of the INS. But for those with less experience and endurance, these cross-country entries often lead to severe dehydration, sunstroke, and often death. Drownings are also common—eighty-seven deaths in 1988—for those who attempt crossing the 164-foot-wide All-American Canal, which courses through the blistering desert near Yuma, Arizona.

Drownings are also frequent along the Rio Grande. Suddenly finding themselves in water over their head or in swift current, the immigrants often panic, and their bloated bodies later turn up downstream. In 1989, 117 drowning victims were recovered from the banks of lower Rio Grande, of whom fifty-three were never identified.[93] Lately, however, freeway crossings claim more victims than river and canal crossings. Between 1987 and 1991, 127 immigrants died and ninety-six more were injured trying to scurry across Interstate 5 in San Diego County.

What most of these immigrants have in their minds as they prepare to cross the border are not the physical risks but their prospects for avoiding the Border Patrol, commonly known as *La Migra*. In the major twin cities, women and men—sometimes entire families—stop at the line that marks the last of Mexico, reviewing their strategies before this critical stretch of their journey. Getting to the other side of the border fence is usually no problem. Usually there are convenient holes cut into the fence or sometimes dug under it. On the outskirts of some cities there are gashes large enough to drive a truck through—and sometimes people do. The informal economy prevails at *la linea*: Vendors sell plastic bags to keep feet dry at shallow river and canal crossings, human *mulas* will carry people across, microentrepreneurs sell hot dogs and burritos for the last meal in Mexico, and for a small fee scouts will check ahead for signs of the Border Patrol.

In their dark green uniforms and light green Chevy Blazers, Border Patrol members wait—and then strike, putting the EWIs (Entering Without Inspection) in the back of their "war wagons" and taking them to the *corralón* (corral) for processing. For those who see this drama for the first time, it shocks, absorbs, amazes, and disgusts. It is a tragedy of human relations, but there is also a comic aspect, especially if one is not part of the action. Looking from the downtown bridge between Juárez and El Paso, one can see coiffured and high-heeled young women, probably maquila workers, being floated over to the other side of the Rio Grande channel for a day of shopping and socializing in El Paso. In Tijuana, hundreds of prospective undocumented immigrants line up along the border fence, facing a couple of beleaguered Border Patrol agents who know that most of them will probably make it to their destination. In Nogales, a couple of elderly men, members of the flourishing informal economy, can be seen making regular trips back and forth across the border, carrying bags of aluminum cans for recycling in the United States.

As twilight descends, floodlights flash on at a few popular crossing spots, a sign that the action will continue through the night. Some prefer crossing by cover of night, but others say that it is easier to blend into the crowd and escape the clutches of the Border Patrol during the daytime. With its night goggles amplifying the starlight, the Border Patrol is also ready for the night shift. Overhead Tijuana a Border Patrol helicopter circles, its powerful spotlight scouring the border and looking for large groups trying to make it across. The regulars, those who frequently cross into the United States for jobs and shopping, call the helicopter *el mosco* (the mosquito) for its pesky character and persistent buzzing.

Most residents of the U.S. border cities take little notice of all this activity. A green van screeches around the corner, a Border Patrol agent hops out and scoops up a couple of "illegal aliens," and no one seems to notice. It is part of the accepted background of life on the line. But this type of law enforcement, making some human beings "illegal" outrages an increasingly vocal minority of human rights, church, and immigration activists. Rubén García, who runs the Annunciation House for immigrants in El Paso, said he grew up in El Paso but never noticed that he was living in a virtual police state.[94]

This perception has been borne out by recent human rights reports by Americas Watch and the American Friends Service Committee. In its 1992 report *Brutality Unchecked*, Americas Watch concluded that beatings, rough physical treatment, and verbal abuse by the INS and its agents were routine and that the border agents go beyond apprehending undocumented immigrants to judging and punishing them.[95] According to the AFSC's 1992 report *Sealing Our Borders: The Human Toll*, the Border Patrol's involvement in drug interdiction has "injected a higher level of paramilitary readiness in immigration control," thereby confusing the patrol's mandate.[96]

Such attitudes and practices have resulted in serious injuries and deaths. Between 1980 and 1992 Border Patrol agents shot dozens of people, killing at least eleven and permanently disabling another ten in the San Diego area alone.[97] Particularly appalling is the impunity that has protected implicated Border Patrol agents from prosecution. Americas Watch found the INS was willing "to cover up or defend almost any form of egregious conduct by its agents," including murder, beatings, torture, and sexual abuse.

The brutality against undocumented immigrants, while certainly not justifiable, is understandable to some degree. Border Patrol agents perform a thankless, impossible job. Each day they know that they will be able to catch only about a third of those crossing the border illegally, and almost all of those detained will eventually make it safely into the United States. Low morale and frustration combined with the increase of violence by drug traffickers and border bandits contribute to their often brutal response.

The state-of-siege mentality that characterizes the INS is in part a product of the increasing number of illegal immigrants it incarcerates rather than simply deposits on the other side of the border, as it usually does with Mexicans without a criminal record. As the number of OTMs (Other Than Mexicans) has risen, the INS has steadily increased the size of its detention centers, which are filled with Haitians, Central Americans, and other OTMs whose deportation often drag on for months. As the U.S. General Accounting Office (GAO) reported in 1992, the number of "criminal aliens" requiring detention has increased dramatically while the "flow [of OTMs] has become a torrent" in recent years.[98]

Crime is a serious problem along the border—both for the migrants themselves and for the communities that hug the border. In San Diego approximately one quarter of those arrested for auto theft and burglary are undocumented persons.[99] Most of the crime by the undocumented, however, is committed not by the millions of undocumented people seeking work in the United States or even by the *coyotes* who guide them across the border but by what police call "the rob-and-return bunch" and the "border bandits."[100]

As one researcher noted, "Despite the awareness that migrant workers as a group are not responsible for much serious crime, police nevertheless lump the crimes committed by this group—'public order misdemeanors' and nonviolent 'survival crimes'— with the statistics for the major crimes (robbery, rape, and murder) committed by border bandits, usually against the migrant workers themselves."[101] Moreover, the high proportion of "aliens" in INS and border-town jails does not necessarily reflect an equally high proportion of alien crimes. Although certainly a matter of concern for border communities, the extent of alien crime may actually be less than commonly believed since the undocumented resident is more likely to be arrested and held without bail than a citizen. Although the extent of immigrant crime may be exaggerated and most immigrants unfairly stereotyped as criminals, there is no denying that crime by undocumented immigrants—those labeled EWIs—has increased dramatically and has become an acute concern for border communities. As a result, some citizen coalitions are calling for stricter immigration-law enforcement and new barriers at the border (ditches, walls, floodlights, etc.) to obstruct the illegal flow.

In the heated public debates along the border over what to do about cross-border crime, there is little attention to or concern about crime committed against undocumented residents of their communities. Generally such crime goes unreported, mostly because of the fear of victims that they will be deported but also because of the widespread distrust and fear that most Mexicans and Central Americans have of the police. A Border Patrol information officer estimated that nine of every ten crimes committed against undocumented people are left unreported.[102]

Symptomatic of the rising border tensions was the 1990 emergence in San Diego County of a citizen program to stop the flow of immigrants. Organizers of the "Light Up the Border" campaign called on supporters to park their cars in strategic areas while training their high beams on the border. The hundreds of people who gathered on the hills and in the canyons of northeast Tijuana each evening waiting to dash into the United States faced yet another obstacle to reaching *el otro lado*. Although frightening, the lights of some 500 cars were not able to turn the tide of this determined immigrant force, proving no more ominous than the INS helicopters circling overhead, the threat of border bandits, or the deep fear of passing unprotected into a foreign land.

The "Light Up the Border" campaign was only one case of a nativist backlash against the economic and political refugees streaming into the United States from the south. More alarming was the appearance of vigilante squads, ranging from the Ku Klux Klan to a group of skinheads called the White Aryan Resistance, that began patrolling the border. Such organized citizen immigration-control efforts proved short-lived but they created a climate in which the abuses of immigrants multiplied. In north San Diego County, an agricultural area where many migrant workers live in appalling squalor in narrow canyons that skirt the coast, the backlash has assumed shocking dimensions. In January 1990 a Carlsbad, California, store owner and his brother, tired of Mexicans loitering around his store, bound Candido Gayoso with duct tape, put a paper bag with no holes over his head, and wrote on the bag *no más aqui* (no more here) as a warning. Aficionados of war games have hunted undocumented immigrants with paint bullets, but there have also been numerous cases of real shootings simply because the gunmen did not like Mexicans.

As if to assure border residents that the government is on their side, the Army Corps of Engineers announced plans in 1992 to mount searchlights on more than 150 concrete poles, each some sixty feet high, along thirteen miles of the California border below San Ysidro. The plan gratified immigration-control activists but alarmed those concerned that the border is turning into a war zone. Another ominous sign was the construction by army reservists of a steel wall along the same stretch of border, replacing the highly porous chain-link fence. Defying immigrants to cut holes in this mother of all fences, the new twelve-foot-high rust-colored barrier is made of 180,000 metal sheets originally intended for use in the Persian Gulf War to establish temporary landing fields in the desert sands. Much to the dismay of the Border Patrol, deter-mined immigrants have met this challenge, successfully cutting through, digging under, and climbing over the steel barrier.

Chapter 3

The Search for an Immigration Policy

The latest U.S. attempt to restrict illegal immigration from Mexico, the 1986 Immigration Reform and Control Act (IRCA), strengthened the shift from temporary to permanent immigration. The product of nearly two decades of legislative wrangling, IRCA made two dramatic changes in immigration law: It imposed sanctions on the employers of undocumented migrants, and it granted legal status to more than three million qualifying undocumented immigrants.[103]

Both these changes contributed to the permanence of Mexican immigrants. First, employer sanctions made it somewhat more difficult for undocumented immigrants to find jobs. This meant that once immigrants had secured positions, they were less likely to leave them for a long trip home. This in turn meant it was preferable to bring family members illegally to the United States than to visit in Mexico. Second, the legalization of the status of 2.3 million Mexicans in the United States increased their security and their ability to house and support undocumented family members.

IRCA's employer sanctions provision developed from the recognition that preventing immigrants from finding jobs when they arrived at their destinations was a key to reducing illegal immigration. Until IRCA, it was illegal for undocumented immigrants to reside in the United States, but it was legal to employ them.[104] Not surprisingly, many employers—especially those in seasonal and labor-intensive businesses like vegetable farming and construction—took advantage of this situation to hire undocumented workers, almost all of whom came from Mexico.

One obvious reason for hiring Mexican workers is that their fear of deportation makes them unlikely to defend their rights in the case of abuses of wage or occupational health and safety laws. Some employers also believed that undocumented workers were less likely to join a union. That labor and human rights abuses are widespread is clear from the number of complaints filed by undocumented workers and their advocates, despite the threat of being returned to Mexico. The Los Angeles-based Center for Human Rights and Constitutional Law reported in 1992 that "in our experience representing thousands of [undocumented] workers, approximately 25 percent are paid below the legal minimum wage, they are regularly penalized (including arrests and deportation) for engaging in union activities to improve working conditions, over 35 percent work under conditions which violate health and safety laws . . . , women are often subject to sexual abuse, and instances of physical beatings and other anti-Mexican 'hate crimes' are on the rise."[105]

But research has shown that the most important reasons for hiring undocumented workers are not related to their legal status so much as to their relatively low expectations of working conditions and job benefits. Over the years immigrants have proved willing to perform hard labor in uncomfortable settings and to work temporarily with no job security. These characteristics, employers argue, mean that undocumented workers do jobs that legal residents will not do, and that therefore they do not take jobs away from citizens. In fact, the argument continues, undocumented workers actually *save* jobs for legal residents by keeping companies profitable that would otherwise go under.

Numerous mainstream economic analyses support the idea that undocumented labor makes a positive contribution to the national economy. They argue that even if some displacement of U.S. workers *does* occur, the low wages and high productivity of undocumented workers mean cheaper goods and services for consumers. Cheap foreign labor also means a more efficient economy overall, greater investment, and eventually jobs for those who were displaced.[106]

Union officials and many labor economists dispute this view of the impact of undocumented workers on the U.S. economy. They suggest that the proper question is not "Who would do these jobs in the absence of illegal immigrants?" but "What would these jobs look like if employers had to hire legal employees?" Those companies competing directly with firms in other nations might well find themselves forced out of business by having to pay higher wages or offer steadier jobs. Light manufacturing and some seasonal agriculture are industries in this position. But many—probably most—undocumented workers are employed in other areas, such as food service, retailing, construction, and temperate-climate agriculture, which face little or no international competition.[107]

In those sectors somewhat insulated from international competition, employers would be forced to automate, restructure, and/or improve wages and working conditions. But since all employers would face the same labor shortage, none would be undercut by competitors' employing cheap labor. Effectively prohibiting the hiring of undocumented workers might slightly increase the cost of certain goods and services, but the amounts would be barely noticeable: Only five cents of the price of a head of lettuce goes to farm workers, for example, so a 20 percent wage hike would add a penny to the cost.[108] And proponents of ensuring that employers hire only documented workers argue that there is a moral dimension to economics, and that efficiency should be balanced by equity. Protecting the rights and the jobs of those at the lowest end of the economic scale makes sense morally and in terms of long-term political stability.

A more fundamental criticism of the mainstream perspective that undocumented immigration has a positive economic effect attacks the theory itself as irrelevant to the real world. Mainstream economists use models that assume full employment, a smooth labor market, and no racial discrimination. The fact that none of these assumptions holds—and certainly not in the lower-income areas where new migrants tend to settle—means that immigrants compete directly with a pool of low-wage and unemployed workers who face great obstacles in finding replacement jobs if they lose out. In this case the benefits of greater economic "efficiency" go exclusively to employers, and tension is created between the new settlers and the groups—often largely African-American—with which they compete.[109]

The debate over immigrants, jobs, and the economy stymied IRCA's predecessor bills for eighteen years. Employers pressured their representatives to stop any law that would endanger their access to temporary low-wage immigrant labor. Unions and immigrant-rights groups opposed any bill that might lead to increased abuse of labor laws and of undocumented workers. Hispanic leaders joined employers in opposing penalties for hiring undocumented workers, fearful—with some reason, it turned out—that employers would discriminate against foreign-looking job applicants in order to protect themselves against prosecution.[110]

In the end employers were given a big loophole: They had to "knowingly hire" an undocumented worker to be subject to penalties. This meant that any decently forged document could be accepted by employers as proof of legality. In addition, farm employers were assured a supply of low-wage, flexible labor by the creation of two new immigration categories: Special Agricultural Workers (SAWs) and Replenishment Agricultural Workers (RAWs). SAW status was to be granted to immigrants who had worked at least ninety days during 1986 or at least ninety days during both 1984 and 1985. The number of applicants far exceeded expert predictions, and studies of farm employment data indicate that at least half the SAW applications were almost surely fraudulent.[111] RAWs were intended to supplement SAWs if the U.S. Department of Labor certified a farm labor shortage, but this provision was never put into effect.

The SAW and RAW provisions were a large part of IRCA's second major change, legalizing the status of certain qualifying immigrants. But the legalization debate had focused largely on IRCA's "amnesty" provision, which offered legal status to people who had illegally entered the country before January 1982 and could show they had lived here until at least May 1987 with only brief absences. Mexicans submitted 1,229,016 applications for legalization, nearly all of which were accepted.

The amnesty provision responded not to the debate over jobs but to the broader question of the effect of undocumented immigrants on U.S. society. For many, the presence of millions of "illegals" represents a loss of national sovereignty because of their violation of the country's borders. Immigrants are also seen as a threat to the U.S. national character. It is argued that there are too many to assimilate effectively into the American way of life and that their proximity to Mexico means that they retain ties that other immigrants have to cut upon arrival.

Others feel that the undocumented population represents a time bomb of social unrest that is fueled by the labor and human rights abuses the foreigners are subject to. Compounding the problem for undocumented immigrants are their lack of trust in and access to the legal system. In the 1980s, these concerns were fed by evidence of rapidly increasing illegal crossings—both from Mexico and Central American nations—and what turned out to be exaggerated estimates of the total number of undocumented immigrants living in the United States.

Most estimates of illegal crossings are based on the number of people apprehended by the INS, which runs the Border Patrol. In 1980 the INS reported 910,361 apprehensions; in 1986 this figure peaked at 1,767,400. The INS estimates that two to three persons are successful in entering the country for every one person who is caught, and that between 90 and 95 percent of those apprehended are Mexicans. These figures mean that estimates for the total number of Mexicans illegally entering the United States increased from roughly 2.5 million in 1980 to roughly four million in 1986.

But calculating what fraction of these undocumented entrants stayed in the United States was much more difficult, so estimates of the population of undocumented immigrants were subject to much greater political manipulation. In 1976, for example, INS commissioner Leonard Chapman told the U.S. Senate that some four to twelve million foreigners resided illegally in the United States. He later wrote that the number of undocumented Mexicans was roughly six million. The actual number was probably less than two million, since five studies by academics and researchers at the U.S. Census Bureau estimated the total population of undocumented Mexicans in 1980—four years later—at between 1.5 and 2.5 million.[112] Nevertheless, Arthur Corwin, an immigration-control proponent, asserted in 1985 that in 1981 between eight and ten million undocumented foreigners lived here. Extremely high estimates such as these continued to make the news and to be used by legislators in debating IRCA.

By 1991 it was clear that IRCA had failed to stem illegal immigration. The Border Patrol reported apprehending 1.2 million undocumented immigrants that year, nearly as many as in pre-IRCA 1985. In part this failure is due to the inability of the INS to enforce employer sanctions; this in turn is related to the ease with which documents are forged. One highly controversial proposal would create a nationwide, computerized system that could instantly verify an applicant's eligibility to work. According to Daniel Stein, executive director of the Federation of American Immigration Reform (FAIR), "We're moving toward a greater national consensus on the need for a national work document, a national registry of births and deaths, and ultimately a national health-care card, a Social Security card issued at birth, and a national birth certificate."[113] This proposal for a national ID has been attacked as an infringement on the constitutional right to privacy, and as more likely to change how fraud occurs than to eliminate it. According to the INS itself, a computerized ID system would be far too expensive.

The difficulties of enforcing employer sanctions have led many immigration-control proponents to pay more attention to those activists and academics who argue that the only long-term answer is the economic development of Mexico. Presidents Bush and Salinas made use of this argument to support the conclusion of the North American Free Trade Agreement (NAFTA). Such an agreement, they argued, would generate economic growth in Mexico, producing jobs and raising wages so that Mexicans would have less reason to emigrate.

Although pleased with the attention being paid to the root cause of Mexican-U.S. migration, many immigration observers are skeptical that free trade is the answer. In the short term, the economic and social changes stemming from the adoption of NAFTA would likely produce a rapid increase in migration, as hundreds of thousands of small farmers and their families are forced out of work by imports of much cheaper corn and other grains from the United States and Canada.[114] In the long term, even if NAFTA does produce more jobs than it eliminates in Mexico, it is unlikely that foreign investment and trade alone could boost economic growth to the levels needed to absorb the million or more workers entering the Mexican labor market each year. It has been estimated that the Mexican economy would have to expand at the rate of 6 percent or more annually to absorb new workers.[115] But it should be remembered that even when the Mexican economy was growing at 6 percent per year from 1945 to 1980, migration continued apace.[116] The boom in foreign investment in the maquila industry did little to halt emigration in the 1980s. Furthermore, the current plan for NAFTA includes no provisions for improving labor standards, so that Mexican wages and working conditions are very likely to remain far below those in the United States and Canada.

Another source of skepticism toward claims that NAFTA will reduce long-term migration is an alternative view of migration that traces the root cause to social linkages between advanced and developing countries and to the disruption of traditional lifestyles. Both trade and foreign investment work to reduce the cultural gap between countries, making immigration easier to contemplate, as international labor specialist Saskia Sassen has observed.[117] A free-trade agreement would accelerate both the process of social integration between the United States and Mexico and the disintegration of Mexico's traditional patterns of work and life. Both these effects can be expected to increase the flow of migrants from Mexico to the United States.[118]

On a more fundamental level, fair-trade activists questioned the exclusion of labor-related questions from the NAFTA negotiations. Why should the conditions under which goods and capital cross borders be discussed, but not those surrounding the movement of workers? Why not address the question directly, instead of hoping for an indirect resolution through investment and growth? Jorge Bustamante, Mexico's leading authority on immigration, has long questioned U.S. motives for not negotiating a bilateral solution to the immigration problem. According to Bustamante, "For us, this thing about the U.S. losing control of the border is kind of a joke. They don't want to have control of the border. It would be uneconomic."[119] In his view, undocumented immigrants should be called "commodity immigrants" since they constitute a self-transportation of labor as a commodity to where the capital owner demands it. Pointing to widespread violation of immigrant rights in the United States, the Salinas administration briefly advocated that immigration and labor mobility issues be discussed within the framework of the free trade agreement.

For the most part, however, calls by progressives for "open borders" for migrant flows, and demands by Mexican leaders for binational immigration accords ignore the social and economic challenges that increasing immigration from Latin America represents for the United States. Recognizing that realistic, not utopian, solutions are needed, some U.S. Latino leaders have started discussing the possibility of a new temporary worker program. Unlike the *bracero* program, the new program would extend beyond the agricultural sector and would ensure that worker's rights to organize and receive the U.S. minimum wage would be respected. Unfortunately no national group has formulated and proposed a specific plan for such an international agreement on migration. Memories of the abuses stemming from the *bracero* program remain vivid, leading most immigrant advocates to shy away from any similar contractual agreement.[120] Community activists, immigrant-rights groups, and labor unions are making admirable efforts to organize undocumented workers, to inform immigrants of their rights, and to enforce those rights in court. But few of these groups are truly interested in pursuing the questions of how to discourage illegal immigration or how to enforce immigration limitations.

The same is true of the Mexican government, which has declined to discuss the possibility of controlling immigration flows either through a program of economic incentives or through a law-enforcement program to limit migrant flows across its northern border. Unless a migration agreement includes completely open borders, some restriction on border crossings and an enforcement mechanism will always be necessary.

Although unpalatable and complex, the need to control U.S. borders and to manage cross-border labor flows must form part of an alternative policy proposal. To ignore them is to assure continued widespread U.S. fears of an uncontrolled "invasion," continued scapegoating of undocumented workers as causing economic hardship, and continued abuse of immigrants' human and labor rights.

Chapter 4

The Drug Connection

The long, mostly open border between the United States and Mexico invites all types of transboundary relationships. Along with migrants, tourists, winter vegetables, manufactured goods, and pollutants, there is trade in *mercancia noble*, contraband. From car stereos and microwave ovens to marijuana, heroin, and cocaine, the porous border permits a bustling, crossboundary trade that falls outside the law.

In the case of drugs, this trade undermines governing structures, fuels violent crime, distorts vulnerable economies, and bolsters well-organized and well-armed interests whose tools for influencing the authorities range from bribery to murder. To get a handle on these problems and on the social disruption of drug abuse, the United States and Mexico have over the years mounted a number of on-again, off-again initiatives. Relishing an on-again stage over the past few years, the two countries are lauding the productive and cooperative relations of the upgraded, binational drug war. Lurking behind the friendly rhetoric, however, the drug trade continues to flourish. It is fed by the same ingredients that helped it grow to its current stature: astounding profits, Mexico's economic needs, the unquenchable U.S. demand for drugs, and a history of backdoor trading relationships that laid the infrastructure for the current drug traffic.

Contrabandistas have traveled the isolated canyons, dusty roads, and shallow waterways of the U.S.-Mexico border since the 1800s. Capitalizing on the legal, geographic, and cultural differences between the two countries, the smugglers have crisscrossed the border, providing consumers in each country with goods not readily available—or legally restricted—on their own side of the line.

During the Civil War, for instance, steamboats puffe(
Rio Grande into the little ports that dotted the river to

with Confederate cotton. They were supposed to head overseas with the cargo and bring back foreign exchange for the Confederacy. But they often never made it that far. Instead they funneled cotton into Mexico, lining the pockets of the traders with riches they poured into fancy homes along the "Gold Coast" in what is now the infamous—and still dirt-poor—Starr County, Texas.[121]

In the twentieth century, Prohibition and the Mexican Revolution stimulated another burst of illicit trade. Thirsty *gringos* who could care less about federal restrictions paid hard cash for bootlegged Mexican liquor and a powerful cactus moonshine called *sotol*.[122] About the same time, U.S. traffickers were funneling weapons and ammunition to revolutionary factions in northern Mexico. And during World War II, many Mexicans with an entrepreneurial spirit headed north with loads of tires, coffee, and other goods that were rationed or just unavailable in the United States.

Nowadays the contraband that most preoccupies U.S. and Mexican officials is drugs. But drugs are not the only goods that have been peddled back and forth between the two countries in recent years. Until Mexico liberalized its import policies, entrepreneurs with a little front money and a vehicle with some cargo space also transported *fayuca*—black-market electronic equipment, appliances, and other consumer goods. Car stereos, VCRs, whiskey, and bolts of fabric were shuttled into Mexico on cargo planes. Stolen cars were—and still are—driven down to Mexico in large numbers. There they are sold, given away as bribes, or used in drug trafficking. Before Mexico eased its import restrictions, even medical and dental equipment found its way to Mexican practitioners who could not or would not wade through the bureaucratic red tape required for import authorization.[123] Up from Mexico came fake Rolex watches, Levi's, designer jeans, folk crafts, and counterfeit money. With the new trading rules, such traffic has slowed considerably, but U.S.-bound runners still smuggle semiprecious metals, archaeological artifacts, and exotic birds.

Unauthorized traffic in such merchandise represents merely lost tax revenues to the U.S. and Mexican governments, but trade in illegal drugs is increasingly seen as a national security threat in both countries. Under the Salinas and Bush administrations, the two countries sharply stepped up their drug control efforts, responding in part to an upsurge in drug traffic from Mexico during the mid-1980s. But controlling the flow of substances such as marijuana, heroin, and cocaine is not a new aspect of U.S.-Mexico relations. It has been an objective of binational policies for decades, achieving greater or lesser importance depending on the volume of drugs crossing the border and the intensity of U.S. concern.

Ebb and Flow of the Mexican Connection

Ironically the modern, illegal drug trade between the United States and Mexico began back in the 1800s as a legal transaction. Marijuana, which grows wild in Mexico, was long considered a traditional folk drug in that country. In the nineteenth century the intoxicating weed was welcomed into the United States, which was then experimenting with a pharmacopoeia of unregulated, narcotics-laced medicines for a variety of ailments. Unwary of the habit-forming effects of some of these substances, the medical profession promoted, and Americans freely purchased, opiates, coca-based products, and marijuana.[124]

Because of its proximity and availability, Mexican marijuana virtually monopolized the U.S. market, and Mexican exports of marijuana and heroin were legal until Mexican President Plutarco Elias Calles banned them in 1927.[125] Even so, small-scale shipments of marijuana continued to flow into the United States through the 1950s. This traffic caused no friction between the two governments, however, possibly because marijuana consumption by that time was largely concentrated among Mexican-origin populations in the United States.[126] The ballooning demand for drugs in the United States during the 1960s pushed Mexican production of marijuana to new heights. By 1975 cheap Mexican pot was meeting nearly 90 percent of the U.S. demand.

Besides marijuana, Mexico is a major producer of heroin for the U.S. market. Opium poppies rode the rails into Mexico at the turn of the century, brought in by Chinese laborers building the country's railway system. Adapting well to the mountainous regions in northern Mexico, the poppy was cultivated in Sonora, Chihuahua, Sinaloa, and Durango. The smokable form of opium became so popular that "opium dens" sprang up in urban centers like San Francisco and Ciudad Juárez. Processed into morphine and heroin, the drug supplied a small market in Mexico—which stimulated Mexican government concerns about addiction as far back as the 1920s—but most was shipped to the United States.[127]

Unlike marijuana, Mexican heroin served only a small portion of the U.S. market, as most consumers preferred the more potent and readily available products smuggled in from Italy, France, Asia, and the Middle East.[128] World War II, however, cut off traditional sources and simultaneously created a need for morphine to treat wounded soldiers. With official U.S. encouragement, the Mexican government legalized the production of opium to meet the needs of the U.S. military. After the war, when traditional suppliers muscled their way back into the business, Mexican "brown" heroin mostly supplied addicts in the U.S. southwest. Only when the "French Connection" was severed in the early 1970s did Mexican heroin enter the U.S. market in force. From a 10 to 15 percent market share in 1972, Mexican "brown" claimed a full 87 percent of the U.S. market by 1975.[129]

Mexico beefed up its eradication programs during the 1970s and brought production of opium poppies back under control. Renewed foreign competition also helped edge Mexican heroin out of the U.S. market. Mexico began a wide-scale aerial eradication program aimed at marijuana, while traffickers in prime growing areas like Colombia and Jamaica began shipping high-potency marijuana such as "Colombian gold" and "ganja" to eager U.S. buyers. Just as important, the Mexican government began spraying large marijuana fields with paraquat, a dangerous herbicide that can cause permanent lung damage. The move, highly publicized by the U.S. media, drew fire in Congress and from the U.S. public because of the potential for harm to U.S. consumers. It also temporarily shattered the U.S. market for Mexican pot, which could be cut and sold before the herbicide had a chance to kill off the leaves, endangering unwary smokers.

The combination of these factors sharply reduced the amount of drugs entering the United States from Mexico. Going into the 1980s, Mexico was supplying about a quarter of the U.S. market for heroin. Likewise, in 1980 less than 10 percent of the marijuana consumed in the United States came from Mexico.[130] Since cocaine had not yet become widely popular in the United States, the drug trade receded as a priority issue in U.S.-Mexico relations.

But not for long. Mexico's economic collapse of the early 1980s coincided with favorable weather conditions, an expanding U.S. market for drugs, and a burst of consumer interest in cocaine. Production and trafficking of opiates and marijuana increased accordingly, and by the mid-1980s these drugs were reclaiming Mexico's market share in the United States. Despite several decades of eradication programs and an intensified antidrug program over the past few years, Mexico is a top supplier of drugs to the United States in the early 1990s. The National Narcotics Intelligence Consumers Committee estimates that more than 70 percent of the foreign marijuana consumed in the United States during 1991 came from Mexico.[131] Likewise, available evidence suggests that about 20 percent of the heroin used in the United States comes from Mexico, a drop from the 1986-87 high of about 40 percent.[132] What's more, most of the heroin provided by Mexico is now a potent variety known as "black tar."

The 1980s saw another trend develop in U.S.-Mexico drug relations: the use of Mexico as a major transshipment route for South American cocaine. Mexico does not grow coca or produce cocaine, but it has been a transit route for cocaine for as long as there has been a market for it in the United States. Demand for cocaine surged in the United States in the 1980s, stimulating increased traffic through Mexico. Also pushing Mexico into a transshipment role was the U.S. crackdown on cocaine traffic through the Caribbean and the southeastern United States. Mexico's long, undefended border with the United States attracted South American cocaine cartels that found entry through their more traditional routes obstructed by U.S. interdiction operations. By the 1990s it was estimated that more than half of the cocaine entering the United States passed through Mexico first.[133]

Big Money in Hard Times

Vast sums of money drive the drug trade. As of 1989, the U.S. State Department reported that a full 60 percent of the world's illegal drug supply was consumed in the United States.[134] In 1986 the U.S. House of Representatives Select Committee on Narcotics Abuse and Control estimated that the value of the drug trade in the United States could be as high as $110 billion, although others put the total closer to $60 billion.[135] Even the lower figure is staggering, but if the higher sum is accurate, the money poured into the U.S. drug trade exceeded 2 percent of the U.S. gross domestic product at the time of the study. Other comparisons are just as startling. If the committee was on target, the amount U.S.

citizens spent on drugs in the mid-1980s represented twice what the United States paid for oil, half of U.S. military expenditures, and about three-quarters of the Mexican gross national product.[136]

Reliable figures on the money involved in the drug trade are as difficult to get in Mexico as they are in the United States. In 1991, however, Jorge Tello Peón, chief of the "crimes against health" department of the Mexican attorney general's office, gave a jarring estimate of the value of the trade in Mexico. He said that traffickers in Mexico were earning nearly as much as the country's total export earnings.[137]

These huge dollar flows are especially crucial during times of economic downturn, when the juxtaposition of poverty and profit spurs more people to take part in the illicit economy. Production and trafficking centers often are located in communities where economic opportunities are rare. Isolated growing areas friendly to poppies and marijuana or proximity to the border and a network of drug-running contacts are the only assets some communities can boast.

Even though some 90 percent of the value of illegal drugs is added in the United States at the wholesale and retail levels, growing marijuana and opium poppies nets Mexican *campesinos* far more cash than cultivating legal crops.[138] When Mexico's economy went into its tailspin in 1982, drug production climbed. Small-scale farmers produce the majority of the marijuana and opium poppies grown in Mexico, and after *la crisis*, marijuana and poppy plots cropped up more frequently alongside fields of corn and beans grown by subsistence farmers. Intercropping with legal crops had been common since the 1970s, partly because the Mexican government is reluctant to spray herbicides on such plots owing to the political and human costs that result when the spray drifts onto food crops. But the increased production of illegal drugs by *campesinos* also reflected the stranglehold poverty had on Mexico's rural population. In 1987, the U.S. State Department's Bureau of International Narcotics Matters pointed to Mexico's economic stagnation and high inflation rate as serious push factors behind *campesino* production of illicit crops: "Financial rewards for a peasant to grow marijuana or opium poppy far outweigh those to be received through cultivating legitimate crops. Peer pressure from other peasants growing illicit crops adds to the incentive. Even peasants who work the fields of others growing such crops earn at least twice the prevailing minimum wage. Thus, the growing of narcotics represents a buffer from the economic crisis."[139]

What the State Department found in 1987 paralleled the reality that existed a full decade before. At that time a *campesino* in the Sierra Madre could earn about $400 a year raising traditional crops. By growing opium poppies, however, that income climbed to between $2,000 and $4,000 dollars.[140] In view of inflation, inadequate credit, periodic drought, and the paltry size of peasant landholdings, the money from drug production offered welcome relief to many poor *campesinos*.

Grinding rural poverty still plagues small farmers in Mexico. In fact, social disruption and economic pressure from free-market reforms have intensified in rural areas, fueling the tendency to grow illicit crops as a household survival strategy. According to the U.S. State Department, that is one explanation for the expansion of drug-producing areas in Mexico, even in the face of enhanced eradication and interdiction programs. Whereas the tristate region of Sinaloa, Durango, and Chihuahua remains the primary source of most illegal drugs from Mexico, the area devoted to regular cultivation of these crops has grown over the years. A significant amount of marijuana for export is now produced in Jalisco, San Luis Potosí, Sonora, Zacatecas, Chiapas, Guerrero, Michoacán, and Oaxaca.[141]

Opium poppy cultivation has also expanded. Once largely confined to Sinaloa, Durango, Chihuahua, and Guerrero, opium poppies are now grown in a zone that starts at the northern tip of the Sierra Madre Occidental in Sonora and Chihuahua and continues down to Chiapas and the Guatemalan border. As the State Department explains, "Adverse agricultural and economic conditions have forced farmers in nontraditional areas to turn to cultivating illicit crops."[142]

Not only *campesinos* find work in the drug trade. *La droga* spawns a multifaceted industry, requiring a wide range of skills and employees. Those who produce and process the drugs are only the first links in the chain. Someone must package the product. Others devise and craft the contraptions—like hollow fence posts or hidden compartments in propane tanks—in which the substances are concealed. Bodyguards, "enforcers," and armed squads protect the shipments, guard the ringleaders, and make sure people pay up or otherwise follow through on their commitments. There are "mules" to run the drugs across the border;

there are lookouts, drivers, and pilots. Some of the most sophisticated organizations rely on communications experts to set up
secure phone lines and radio hookups to their sources, distributors, and partners. And of course, there are accountants, money
launderers, and in some cases actual financial advisers. The unemployed are common recruits for the less skilled of these jobs, and the
incomes they make from drug-running can have a dramatic effect on
shaky economies. In a little place like Douglas, Arizona, the fifteen
hundred dollars a driver makes running a load of dope to Tucson
can make a big difference to local businesses. As one observer described the economic effects of the drug trade on a small town along
the south Texas border, "The drivers are all unemployed, but after
two weeks they're buying pickups and ostrich-skin cowboy boots
with matching belts. Pretty soon there's money all around town. The
car dealers are selling trucks, gas sales go up, so do groceries and
clothes. The bank deposits are up—but no one says anything. And
no taxes are paid. It creates a false economy."[143]

Aside from the employment networks, there are investments.
Because of the illegality of the trade, there are no figures describing the extent of these investments or their impact on local economies. Most observers, in fact, question the real effect of drug
money in Mexico, pointing to the diversified nature and large size
of the economy as factors that tend to dilute the significance of
drug revenues. But drug money is invested in Mexico—and in the
United States. It is known that traffickers have put money into
tourist hotels, restaurants, movie theaters, shopping centers, and
luxury homes. "The traffickers are the only ones investing money
in Mexico," a Mexican businessman complained to a reporter in
1986. "The rest take their dollars out. They are building roads,
drainage, restaurants, and hotels, which creates jobs."[144]

Real estate booms and bank deposit surpluses in places like
Mazatlán, Durango, Phoenix, and San Diego are fed in part by
drug money, although the size of their economies hides the full
extent of trafficker involvement. In some communities, however,
the drug trade involves wide sectors of the population and leaves
visible marks on the economy. One observer estimated that some
15 to 20 percent of the population in the Sonoran border town of
Agua Prieta depended on drugs in 1991, a trend that began in the
early 1980s.[145] During its drug-running heyday in the mid-1980s,
the "Gold Coast" in Starr County, Texas, boasted million-dollar

homes and Mercedes cars bought with cash in an area where half the work force was unemployed.[146] In 1990 a controversial study in Douglas, Arizona, sampled residents and found that they believed 30 to 60 percent of the town's economy was based on the drug trade.[147]

But profits from the drug trade do not have the strong multiplier effect these examples suggest. As with junk bond speculation and other get-rich-quick schemes, drug profits pay for personal consumption more than for productive investments or improvements in infrastructure. Trafficking and production centers tend to show no lasting benefits as a result of the drug trade even though individuals may have profited and helped support the local economy in critical ways. "The big traffickers piss the money away," observed Mike Gallagher, a reporter who has studied the drug trade for nearly two decades. "They buy big cars, they buy elephants and tigers and make zoos on their mountain estates," Gallagher explained. "They may build a clinic or two, but these guys are crooks. They don't care about their communities and add nothing to them."[148]

Networks of Violence

What does have a multiplier effect is the violence. Trafficking in illegal drugs provides the economic backbone for organized crime. A bilateral commission studying U.S.-Mexico relations reported that the drug trade represented almost 40 percent of the economic activity of powerful criminal organizations in the United States.[149] In both Mexico and the United States the strongest of these organizations are vertically structured networks with international links. Most of them are "polydrug" organizations, controlling production, transportation, and wholesale distribution of a number of drugs simultaneously. Their capacity for corrupting officials and imposing their will on society expands along with their profits, presenting immense challenges to elected officials.

Intergang rivalries spill across the border, and trafficking organizations from Sonora and Sinaloa have settled scores with rivals and turncoats in the U.S. as well as in Mexico. Drug-related murders, sometimes accompanied by torture and mutilation, have hit border communities and nearby cities. Execution killings to ensure loyalty and prevent theft within smuggling rings have also become more common in border communities. In 1989, for example, both Tucson and Agua Prieta suffered gruesome execution-style mass murders carried out by groups involved in the drug trade.[150]

The violence is not confined to the border. Mexicans called the mountain city of Culiacán, Sinaloa, "Little Chicago" during the 1970s because the gunfights between rival drug gangs resembled those of Chicago's mobsters during Prohibition. Others thought the Chicago comparison far too generous. "Culiacán," journalist Craig Pyes observed, "has only 350,000 inhabitants and the equivalent of a St. Valentine's Day Massacre every two weeks."[151] By 1986 Culiacán's murder rate climbed to five a day, accompanied by widespread rape and other assaults on the general public. As in some of the inner cities in the United States, residents in Culiacán were afraid to sit near their windows because they feared being struck by stray bullets.[152]

The increased antidrug efforts of the United States and Mexico have not reduced the violence. In 1992, Guadalajara's drug-related murder rate was three per day. Violence is up in Culiacán and in Sonora as well. Quick to fight with the machine guns, hand grenades, and semiautomatics from arsenals purchased with the huge profits of drug sales, traffickers are much better armed than in the 1980s.

The weapons trade worries both the U.S. and Mexican governments, as well as affected communities. Flowing exclusively from north to south, these arms include high-caliber assault weapons and military-issue armaments like grenades, rocket launchers, and, in one case, even a fully armed combat assault helicopter.[153] Trafficker arsenals often have greater firepower and are more sophisticated than those of the military forces and law-enforcement agencies responsible for stemming the drug trade. This is especially so at the local level, where police forces and drug agents in both Mexico and the United States are likely to find themselves outgunned in confrontations with traffickers.

In towns where traffickers hold sway, the weapons contribute to a climate of fear and intimidation that aids corruption and makes a shambles of daily life. In Ojinaga, a dusty border town just a few miles upstream and across the border from Big Bend National Park in Texas, traffickers with AK-47s slung across their shoulders walked the streets in broad daylight as recently as 1987. Shootouts on street corners and at convenience stores, ice-cream stands, and restaurants threatened innocent bystanders and rivals alike, while traffickers received protection from federal agents, local police, and the military in exchange for monthly payoffs.[154]

In addition to these specific forms of violence, trafficking networks have the potential to become alternative centers of power, threatening constitutional structures.[155] To some extent, this distortion of the governing system has already occurred in Mexico. It has been visible in corruption that has sometimes penetrated to top levels of the government and that has riddled certain governing, military, and security structures. Corruption in Mexico has been described as the "glue that holds the Mexican system together and the oil that makes it work." The "oil" makes the "wheels of bureaucracy turn," while the "glue . . . seals political alliances."[156]

Corruption is so much a part of the way things have historically been done in Mexico that bribery, kickbacks, and buyoffs often do not have the unethical taint such deeds acquire in the United States. It is not surprising then that drug-related corruption has penetrated nearly all aspects of Mexico's drug-war machinery at one time or another.[157] In November 1991, for example, an army unit guarding a Colombian drug shipment near Veracruz killed seven Mexican antidrug agents in a shoot-out that lasted nearly three hours.[158]

Aside from being a public embarrassment to the Salinas government—the whole event was videotaped from an antidrug aircraft flying overhead—the involvement of military troops guarding the shipment and early government attempts to downplay the Veracruz incident demonstrated the continued role of corruption in perpetuating the drug trade in Mexico. The Mexican press reported that the November gunfight was the third time over the preceding few months that local military had blocked police from intercepting drug shipments, allowing the traffickers to escape.[159] Not only a threat to antinarcotics efforts, military involvement in trafficking schemes is an internal security issue that jeopardizes government authority as well as law enforcement operations.

Official corruption is compounded by the web of connections between trafficking organizations and some parts of Mexican society. The major Mexican trafficking organizations have historically been dominated by family groups, such as the Herreras who have controlled the most important economic and government functions in the entire state of Durango for four decades.[160] But the family-based operation is gradually being blended with cartel-like organizational structures based on megadollar monetary re-lationships and specialized functions. The Guadalajara cartel, in-volved in the torture-murder of U.S. Drug Enforcement Agent Enrique Camarena, was one of the first examples of this phe-nomenon in Mexico. This form of organization amplifies the power and reach of the trafficking networks, creating the potential for the kind of national disruption and violence seen in Colombia and Peru over the last decade. This potential seems to have been an important factor behind President Salinas's declaration that drug trafficking is a matter of national security in Mexico.

Foundations of the Drug War

Mexico has been conducting its own eradication campaigns since 1948. In the highlands Mexican soldiers met *mano a mano* with mari-juana stalks and opium poppies, beating them with sticks until the fields were mangled piles of weeds. These search-and-destroy mis-sions were reasonably effective, but they failed to keep pace with production. So in 1961 Washington gave Mexico Korean War vintage aircraft and military equipment to use in its *gran campaña* against marijuana and poppy fields.[161] U.S. advisers also went to Mexico to help with drug control efforts. Production continued to climb, how-ever, encouraged by the decade's expanding market for mind-altering substances in the United States.

By 1969 the drug trade and the drug consumption habits of U.S. young people had so annoyed the "law-and-order" admini-stration of Richard Nixon that the United States launched a sur-prise border search-and-seizure effort called Operation Intercept.[162] The three-week operation—which involved searching every vehicle and individual crossing into the United States from Mexico—was intended to squeeze Mexico economically, by snarl-ing legitimate trade and tourist traffic. The operation netted no major drug shipments but did push Mexico into stepping up its own antidrug programs and working with the United States on a joint effort known as Operation Cooperation.[163]

Operation Cooperation ensured the United States had a strong voice in Mexican drug policy, but it failed to put a dent in the rapidly expanding marijuana and opium supply, and U.S. advisers pressed Mexican counterparts to use herbicides against the crops.[164] When

Mexico began an aerial eradication program in 1975, the United States was there with money, advice, and other support.

Washington's financing enabled Mexico to buy or lease U.S. planes and helicopters for the *campaña permanente* against drug crops. Other U.S. aid was provided so that Mexico could construct field air bases, train pilots, and install communications systems.[165] The aircraft, used both for spraying herbicides and transporting troops, were maintained largely with U.S. funding, with maintenance and advisory services provided in part by U.S. corporations.

Mexico's commitment to the eradication campaign was particularly strong for a number of reasons. These ranged from the desire to regain control of highland areas where *campesinos*—receiving their first good incomes ever—were thumbing their noses at Mexico City to concerns about domestic drug abuse to the country's need to maintain good relations with the United States.[166] As a consequence, Mexico's working relationship with U.S. drug-control forces was at an all-time high during the mid- and late 1970s. Information exchanges were numerous, and DEA agents worked closely with Mexican counterparts. Joint investigations of traffickers and their organizations also went forward. By the end of the decade drug control enthusiasts in the United States were pointing to Mexico as a model of antinarcotics policy. Eradication was up, arrests were up, production was down, and Mexico's share of the U.S. drug market plunged.

When the program fell apart at the end of the López Portillo administration, the United States was so used to holding up Mexico as an example of good drug policy that at first U.S. policy makers did not know there was a problem. Although U.S. support for Mexico's aerial eradication program continued, it had dropped to modest levels of annual support—around eight million dollars a year. But the eradication program was suffering from inefficiency, low salaries, maintenance failures, and rising corruption.[167] The new government of Miguel de la Madrid—saddled with an economic disaster and opposed to the Reagan administration's Cold War policy in Central America—did not make the drug fight a high priority. Weather conditions were favorable, and peasants caught in an economic tailspin turned to illicit crops to pull out of it.

The traffickers themselves regrouped, stronger than ever, from the campaigns of the 1970s. Polydrug organizations, sometimes linked in cartel-type structures, funneled heroin, marijuana, and cocaine to the United States. Supported by networks of corruption, some of them—like the Sinaloan traffickers who moved south and became the Guadalajara cartel—became ostentatious, greedy, and overconfident. They began investing in state-of-the-art, multiacre marijuana plantations that were based on agribusiness management and production techniques. Well-irrigated emerald islands popped up even in the Chihuahua desert, with fields worked by campesinos trucked in for premium wages (in Mexican terms) from destitute rural areas miles away. Drug production and trafficking to the United States surged, while cooperation between antidrug forces in the two countries fell off.

These years marked the low point of recent U.S.-Mexico antidrug efforts. Because many other issues drive the U.S.-Mexico relationship, however, the two countries remained on generally decent terms as far as the broader picture was concerned. Problems such as debt management and Washington's strong support for the economic reforms begun under de la Madrid tied the two countries together in powerful bonds that drug control failures could not sever. Washington's pressure on Mexico to get into step with the drug war intensified, and U.S. antidrug assistance climbed, especially after President Reagan signed a secret directive in 1986 declaring the international drug trade a threat to U.S. national security.

After the Salinas and Bush administrations took office, collaboration on drug control activities intensified, and by the early 1990s cooperation between the two countries was at its strongest since the 1970s. Until 1993, in fact, Mexico traditionally received the largest amount of U.S. annual expenditures for foreign drug control. The aid supported all aspects of the drug war, including intelligence collection, eradication, and interdiction. From 1978 to 1990 the State Department's Bureau of International Narcotics Matters (INM) provided $150.3 million to Mexico as assistance for drug-control activities, with more than half of that amount provided after 1986.[168] In 1991, INM contributed nearly $20 million to Mexico, with a similar amount provided in 1992.[169] As with other U.S. government aid programs, however, direct aid to Mexico was cut back in 1993. The INM currently funds only U.S. activities related to the drug war in Mexico, and the Mexican government has picked up its own share of the tab.[170]

The Frictions of Asymmetry

Despite cooperative efforts, the drug trade has been a lasting source of friction between Mexico and the United States, often overshadowing other areas of disagreement such as immigration and foreign policy. Finger pointing and chicken-or-the-egg arguments over the relative influence of U.S. demand versus Mexican supply on stimulating and maintaining drug traffic have been as typical of U.S.-Mexico antidrug relationships as have periods of cooperation. Richard Craig, an expert on the drug trade and drug policy, describes those relations as "cyclical in nature, often unilateral, incident-prone, and highly acrimonious."[171]

As with other policy areas, the tensions of the antidrug relationship stem partly from the overall asymmetry between the United States and Mexico. Although, as noted above, Mexico has its own good reasons for fighting the drug trade, it has pursued antidrug strategies framed mostly by U.S. wishes and needs since the early part of the century.[172] When drug use and abuse surge in the United States, domestic pressures rise to cut off the flow of drugs into the country. If Mexico's share of the U.S. market happens to be high at the time, then the pressure is aimed at Mexico.

Because of the United States' importance as a trading partner and as a source of tourist and investment dollars, Mexico generally responds by cranking up its own antidrug activities. This factor was the main reason the Nixon and Reagan administrations chose in effect to shut down the border through enhanced customs inspections when they wanted to push Mexico toward "cooperation" on the drug war in 1969 and 1985.[173]

In the 1980s U.S. influence grew even greater because Mexico needed Washington's help with debt management strategies and its approval on loans from international financial institutions like the World Bank. That type of much-needed support was directly threatened by U.S. congressional restrictions on aid to countries that did not cooperate "fully" on antinarcotics activities. Because of these restrictions, Mexico had to meet "certification" requirements in order to continue receiving U.S. backing on other economic issues. U.S. presidents and the State Department repeatedly certified Mexico as fully cooperating on antidrug efforts, an assessment that some members of Congress strongly contested until the late 1980s. But the fact that Mexico's drug control activities had to be given a U.S. stamp of approval set off waves of anti-U.S. criticism in Mexico whenever certification time rolled around.

This pattern of U.S. pressure and Mexican compliance—with all its corresponding negative foreign policy effects—results partly from the supply-side focus of U.S. antidrug strategies. Historically U.S. policies put the greatest emphasis on curtailing production and severing trafficking routes in source and transit countries, while neglecting effective prevention and treatment programs to reduce demand at home. To implement international antidrug programs, the United States deploys U.S. drug enforcement agents in supplier countries. United States intelligence agencies float satellites overhead and take surveillance photos of the territories of U.S. allies, sometimes without permission. Washington pushes countries involved in the supply network to draw up laws and devise policies compatible with U.S. antinarcotics objectives. In some places, notably the Andean countries, the United States has even sent its military to join in antinarcotics operations.

Mexico is considered a "crucial component" of U.S. drug control strategies, so the antidrug activities of the United States are especially pronounced there.[174] Beyond its central position in the drug war, "Mexico's economic and geopolitical importance to the U.S. exceeds that of any other drug trafficking/producing country," a State Department memorandum explained in 1991.[175] Responding to these interests, a myriad of U.S. agencies, ranging from the Central Intelligence Agency (CIA), to the Federal Bureau of Investigation (FBI), to the Agency for International Development (AID), have worked on antidrug projects in Mexico. The two countries have worked on eradication and interdiction programs in Mexico's airspace, in its territorial waters, and on its soil. The United States has bolstered its own southern border with military and National Guard forces working with federal, state, and local law-enforcement agencies. Each of these initiatives has produced concern and even resentment in Mexico, where many see such moves as a threat to national sovereignty.

Drawing the greatest fire, however, has been the U.S. Drug Enforcement Administration (DEA). With more than forty agents assigned to Mexico, the DEA's largest foreign operation is conducted on Mexican soil.[176] These agents—who are stationed throughout the country—collect intelligence, share information with Mexican authorities, conduct investigations, and perform most other law-enforcement tasks shy of arrests. But the presence of the DEA on Mexican territory irritates nationalists both in and out of government. As a consequence, the agents are not allowed to carry firearms. An unwritten agreement from the 1920s permits U.S. drug agents to carry their own personal handguns, but if they are stopped by Mexican police and have such weapons in their possession, they can be arrested. In addition, until recently DEA agents were not issued diplomatic credentials. This fact was particularly grating to the agents, who raged in the mid-1980s that even U.S. government personnel working to wipe out the screwworm, a parasite that infests cattle in northern Mexico and southern Texas, carried the black diplomatic passports.[177]

Clearly the combination of U.S. hegemony and Mexican sovereignty issues is a combustible mixture. Periodic explosions in the press and at the diplomatic and agency levels reveal underlying tensions that persist below the surface even during times of cooperation. As noted by Richard Craig, such explosions tend to follow "incidents," such as the murder of Enrique Camarena and the 1990 revelation that a CIA satellite had taken unauthorized surveillance photos of Mexican territory to survey marijuana production.[178]

On occasion, unilateral actions on the part of the United States have also aggravated relations among Mexican and U.S. diplomats and agency personnel trying to conduct bilateral programs. For example, the DEA put bounties on the heads of individuals involved in Camarena's murder and put out the word in the right circles that it wanted the perpetrators brought to the United States to stand trial. Between 1986 and 1992 five kidnappings resulted from the DEA offer, setting off burst after burst of Mexican anger and demonstrating the cowboy approach to international relations for which the United States is so often criticized.[179]

Then, in 1992, the U.S. Supreme Court ruled that U.S. extradition agreements with Mexico did not explicitly prohibit the United States from trying Humberto Alvarez Macháin, one of the suspects in the Camarena case, even though he had been brought to the United States without Mexico's authorization.[180] In one of its strongest moves ever, Mexico reacted by suspending the activities of the DEA on its soil and putting on hold the extradition treaty with the United States. Within days, however, the Salinas government had quietly retracted the decisions and returned to negotiations with the United States over extradition policies, moves that underlined the asymmetry of the relationship and U.S. dominance within it.

Failed Policies

With all these joint efforts and with Mexico's own vastly increased antidrug activities, the drug trade continues to flourish. Record-breaking seizures of cocaine and record numbers of marijuana and poppy plots destroyed since 1990 have not diminished the supply of drugs on the U.S. market. Drugs are readily available on the streets, and, according to the National Narcotics Intelligence Consumers Committee 1991 report, they are still cheap enough and pure enough to satisfy the market. In fact, in the case of cocaine—the drug that most frightens the United States and Mexico—the street price was less in 1991 than it was in 1990, and its potency was increasing, although it was nowhere near as potent as it was in 1988, a reflection of some successful interdiction efforts.

At the same time, the social factors that feed the trade are still in place. Poverty and unemployment limit economic options and encourage citizens in both countries to turn to the drug trade as a survival strategy. Low salaries for most law-enforcement officers are a fact of life on both sides of the border, leading to increased corruption. In Mexico the Salinas government has cracked down on this problem, at some risk to its own popularity among certain circles. But at the state and local levels, some of the forces that have facilitated the drug trade for years are still in place. Many Mexican Federal Judicial Police who are fired for corruption, for example, are simply rehired at the state level.[181]

In the United States, as well, although the problem has been less studied and less reported, corruption is common. And for good reason. Ninety cents of every dollar spent on the drug trade is generated in the United States. That provides an awful lot of cash to buy the services—or the temporary blindness—of law-enforcement officers making civil service salaries.

Huge profits and persistent demand also provide momentum to the drug trade that a few years of intensified drug control programs cannot combat. Although U.S. drug use is down slightly on the whole and down measurably among certain populations, the size of the market is still more than large enough to fuel the multibillion-dollar enterprise of drug trafficking.

Other factors also tend to encourage the drug trade. They are the unintended side effects of U.S.-Mexico trade policies and Mexico's economic reforms since the mid-1980s. The privatization of government-held businesses carried out under Salinas, for example, has provided a flood of reasonably priced enterprises for purchase by legitimate investors and drug dealers alike. According to the State Department's Elizabeth Carroll, some of these businesses are being snapped up by traffickers in order to launder and invest the profits from their drug operations.

Ironically the sweeping antinarcotics efforts of the United States and Mexico are contradicted at least in part by trade-liberalization measures that the governments have worked hard to conclude. If NAFTA is ratified, for example, the border is expected to boom with new development. Up and down the border, new entry stations will open, and on each side, *colonias* and tiny sister cities like Santa Teresa and San Jerónimo on the New Mexico-Chihuahua border are expected to swell with people wanting employment from the trade boom. Roads will be widened, airports constructed, and bridges erected or expanded to handle the hoped-for increase in U.S.-Mexico commercial traffic. If all goes as planned, new businesses will move in, with their eyes trained on markets and business partners that lie across the border. In large population areas already bustling with transboundary movements, each of these trends will be magnified.

This build-up of urban areas will provide nourishing environments for traffickers. Economic growth on each side of the border will spawn a proliferation of bonded warehouses and other industrial sites serving as fronts for drug smuggling, with customs inspectors less likely to scrutinize shipments from such enterprises. Vast amounts of drugs are already spirited into the country in commercial vehicles—hidden in containerized shipments, in false panels beneath crates of oranges and raisins, in boxcars, hidden compartments, and fuel tanks. Customs inspectors—even when they are aided by teams of National Guard troops and sniffer dogs—can only inspect a few of these shipments each day at current traffic loads. Most vehicles are waved through as it is. With the trade increases anticipated over the next few years, the border is likely to be swamped with drugs.

Efforts are already under way to respond to these concerns. Surveillance systems are being upgraded and are becoming more high-tech. Mobile x-ray vans, fiber optics, and portable contra-band detectors are being added to the arsenals of customs inspectors at some border crossings. Tourists returning from a sunny stay on the beaches at Guaymas or truckers hauling Mexican produce may one day pass their vehicles through border x-ray sensors like those at airports. Dope-sniffing dogs already wind their way through lines of waiting vehicles in some U.S. customs lines. National Guard troops hunting for drugs pick through lettuce bins and scour suspicious vehicles for signs of hidden compartments, lending a helping hand to overworked customs agents.

But cracking down too heavily on cross-border traffic in order to stop drugs causes other problems. The affront to Mexican sensibilities is a sharply negative consequence of stepped-up border enforcement, especially because U.S. traffic into Mexico is subject to virtually no inspection whatsoever. Filtering Mexican entrants to the United States through a sieve of surveillance mechanisms sends a bleak message of distrust at the same time the United States is hoping to step up relations with its southern neighbor.

The slow pace of U.S. customs inspections already draws a lot of criticism anyway. Besides the aggravation of delays, produce in unrefrigerated trucks runs the danger of spoilage in the hot sun, and incoming cars and trucks backed up with their engines idling increase air pollution in cities like El Paso and San Diego. In addition, using National Guard troops and canine teams to enhance inspections adds to the appearance—and reality—of border militarization.

For all these reasons, greatly intensified searches at border checkpoints are not likely to be a serious option. Instead, most U.S. and Mexican antidrug activities will probably still focus on eradicating supply within Mexico, interdicting traffickers before they get to the United States, and disrupting trafficking organizations through intelligence and law-enforcement operations.

But persisting with this supply-side law-enforcement orientation has its own drawbacks. For one thing, large-scale, expensive law-enforcement actions tend to rid the playing field of small, weak trafficking organizations but do little to dent the power of the big families and cartels. Such organizations are the only ones strong enough and big enough to adjust to enforcement pressures and even to profit from them. They have the funds needed for hefty bribes, the connections in high places needed to facilitate secure operations, and the sophisticated skills and equipment required to outmaneuver antidrug initiatives. When law enforcement agents clear the field of their competitors, these big organizations are often able to increase their own holdings and magnify the scope of their operations.[182]

Moreover, funneling support to military and police forces in Mexico is a questionable remedy to the drug trade, especially in view of the persistence of corruption and human rights abuses in these institutions. This is especially true given the extent of producing areas and the reliance of many poor and unemployed people on the drug trade for their livelihoods. Law-enforcement and eradication activities are only partial and inadequate solutions that bolster the power of agencies often known for resorting to the heavy hand. In the United States as well, the danger to civil liberties and human rights from drug-control efforts is growing. From random urine testing to strip searches, personal privacy is increasingly threatened. Antidrug agents along the border have even more freedom than most national and state laws allow police agencies. Because many of these agents have been cross-deputized by the DEA and U.S. Customs Service, these forces—whether from customs, police, or immigration agencies—are entitled to do searches without warrant in border communities and inland areas vulnerable to smuggling.

Effective remedies to the drug trade will require more than punitive measures. Pulverizing organized crime interests is one thing; pouring scarce national resources—whether U.S. or Mexican—into an ineffective war against drugs that violates human rights is another. By not considering options beyond militarization and law enforcement, not facing squarely the importance of U.S. demand and its social causes, and not grappling with the poverty that drives many people to join the drug trade, U.S. and Mexican antinarcotics initiatives are themselves doomed to failure.

Chapter 5

Calling in the Troops

National Guard troops searching trucks entering from Mexico, Marine observation posts in the desert, aerial reconnaissance, and joint patrols by the Border Patrol and army troops all are signs of a military buildup along the U.S.-Mexico border. Unlike many other international borders, this militarization is the result not of conflictive binational relations but of heightened U.S. concern that South-North migratory and narcotics traffic is endangering its national security. This one-sided response to these international problems underlines the asymmetry of U.S.-Mexico relations while raising new concerns that the increasing military presence will aggravate existing cross-border tensions and lead to new civil rights violations.

Considering that the U.S.-Mexico border was largely the creation of the land-grabbing Mexican-American War, the international boundary has been mostly free of direct military conflicts between the two countries, especially since the 1920s. The infamous 1916 raid on Columbus, New Mexico, by Pancho Villa marked the beginning of the only serious cross-border military encounter with Mexican forces in the borderlands during this century. General "Blackjack" Pershing's "punitive expeditionary force" of twenty-thousand men spent more than a year in northern Mexico, unsuccessfully hunting down the revolutionary bandit. On the U.S. side of the border, some hundred thousand federalized National Guard troops kept order from Yuma, Arizona, to Brownsville, Texas. By 1919 U.S. control over the region was clearly established. With the creation of the Border Patrol in 1924, the United States had the beginnings of a permanent civilian enforcement presence on the border.

With few exceptions, border control operations over the next decades had more of a civilian law-enforcement nature than a military one. But Operation Wetback, a 1950s action carried out by the Border Patrol and other elements of the Immigration and

Naturalization Service, took a distinctly military approach. The INS was led at the time by an ex-general who had participated in Pershing's expeditionary force, and he recruited other former officers to help with the operation. Using military tactics, the INS carried out the biggest mass roundup and deportation of undocumented Mexicans in U.S. history. Ground units and aircraft herded groups of Mexicans to the border, from where the Mexican government shuttled the deportees into the Mexican interior by train.[183]

The more recent efforts to beef up control over the border started under President Carter. Heightened concern about undocumented migration and drug trafficking prompted the buildup. At that point the military itself was not involved in the border-control operations, but Carter did appoint another ex-general to head the INS, and the administration moved to upgrade Border Patrol equipment and to construct new lengths of chain link fence in high-traffic crossing areas.

By the early 1980s the momentum toward an increased military presence in the borderlands was unmistakable. Dictated by the concerns of the conservative Reagan and Bush administrations, tighter immigration border controls emerged in response to mounting fears about the spread of narcotics and to new anxieties about job loss to "hordes" of immigrants from Central America and Mexico.

As a result, the United States has steadily expanded the role of military and law enforcement agencies in the borderlands. Increasingly these agencies have a common mission that draws on military means to carry out law-enforcement tasks. Using sophisticated communications and surveillance technology, civilian and military forces from federal, state, and local levels have tried to squeeze off the flow of illegal drugs and undocumented immigrants into the United States. Although only partially successful, the scope of this new military presence sounds alarm bells for concerned observers worried about the impact of "militarization" on human and civil rights in the borderlands.

Militarization refers to an approach to law enforcement and border control that relies on military expertise, technology, equipment, facilities, and strategies, as well as personnel.[184] It results in the integration of military and law-enforcement functions and approaches. As Timothy Dunn, a close observer of the process in the borderlands, described it, "It's when cops act like the military and the military act like cops."[185]

At large ports of entry like San Diego, this militarization is most conspicuous. Customs officers with their canine partners zigzag through lines of pedestrians and vehicles passing through the customs station. The dogs sniff out drugs and undocumented immigrants stashed in trunks of cars and other hiding places. National Guard troops inspect cargo for contraband. Mobile x-ray vans and other high-tech detection devices are becoming more commonplace, while just down the way from official entry stations, tall steel barrier walls, chain link fences, and floodlight systems block the illegal traffic by more prosaic means.

Along the many miles of open border, this militarized approach is also evident, although usually less obvious because of the remote nature of the terrain. But bumping into today's border-control operations in the backcountry can be shocking, and even frightening. Many Border Patrol agents carry military-issue M-16s, responding to the increased firepower of drug traffickers. The agents are also authorized to carry personally owned semiautomatic pistols.[186] Marines on reconnaissance exercises, radar balloons hovering overhead, and the whir of helicopters fitted with searchlights and infrared radar systems give the air of a war zone. Infrared body sensors and magnetic footfall detectors, having once been used in Southeast Asia, are now placed along desolate stretches of border, forming a technological front line of defense for the Border Patrol.

Critical to this new military presence on the border have been presidential and congressional initiatives to loosen the restrictions on the involvement of the armed forces in domestic law enforcement. In 1981 the U.S. Congress reformed the law that previously had strictly circumscribed the military's role in domestic activities. It also wrote new legislation on drug and immigration control that included a role for the armed forces in enforcement efforts. Although still restricted from pursuit, interdiction, search, seizure, or arrest, the military was authorized to help detect and monitor suspicious activities along the border, in partnership with law-enforcement agencies.[187]

Congressional appropriations were even more explicit, funding various types of programs designed to integrate military and civilian forces in border law-enforcement activities. Other legal changes throughout the decade progressively loosened restrictions on military involvement in domestic affairs and broadened the role of the military in law-enforcement functions concerning drug and immigration control.[188] A 1986 presidential declaration that the narcotics trade constituted a threat to national security helped Congress justify the legal changes and push border militarization forward. Congress authorized the military to provide "expert advice" to civilian agencies on tactical and technological matters such as surveillance and intelligence gathering. In an attempt to create an effective interagency network devoted to cutting off the flow of illegal drugs, the Department of Defense assumed charge of integrating the command, control, communications, and intelligence assets of the United States.

By 1991 the armed forces could pick from a variety of ways they could help out with antinarcotics activities, many of which overlap with immigration-control efforts. Besides providing training and advice to civilian agencies, the military can conduct aerial and ground reconnaissance operations in the borderlands to gather intelligence and monitor suspicious movements. Indeed, Congress mandated that the military conduct training exercises "to the maximum extent possible" in high-traffic areas like the borderlands. The looser guidelines on military involvement allow the armed forces to carry out drug eradication campaigns and other operations that support law-enforcement programs.

With new legal freedoms like these plus extra funding and the emphasis on border control under the Reagan and Bush administrations, military and law-enforcement functions became increasingly intertwined in the borderlands. The 1986 launching of Operation Alliance—a multiagency law-enforcement initiative targeting the border area—and the subsequent designation of the U.S.-Mexico border as a "High Intensity Drug Trafficking Area" in 1990 pushed these efforts forward. Operation Alliance's mandate is "to foster interagency cooperation and to interdict the flow of drugs, weapons, aliens, currency, and other contraband across the Southwest border."[189] It represents the largest, most ambitious interagency action of its kind ever attempted by the U.S. government.

To plan and coordinate military support for Operation Alliance, the Pentagon created Joint Task Force 6 (JTF-6) in 1989 and stationed the new unit at Fort Bliss in El Paso. Representatives from various branches of the military serve on the task force, which fields requests for support from the civilian agencies and arranges for military participation in their law-enforcement efforts. The National Guard, marines, and army have been especially active in these operations, as have special forces, like the Army Rangers, Green Berets, and paratroopers. Among other things, they offer transportation assistance, deploy and monitor ground radar and seismic sensors, conduct trainings, carry out surveillance and reconnaissance missions, clear brush, build and improve roads, construct and repair fences, provide intelligence, and inspect cargo at border crossings.[190]

One operation coordinated by JTF-6 was a reconnaissance training exercise carried out near Naco, Arizona, in August 1992. Around two hundred marines from Camp LeJeune, North Carolina, set up observation posts and marched on foot patrols fully armed with M-16s. Wearing green greasepaint and camouflage, the troops crept through the tall grass along the border or bounced over rugged terrain in Humvees—the four-wheel-drive vehicles used for conducting motorized patrols. Their task was to practice surveillance and reconnaissance, and all the other skills necessary for a "wartime mission," according to the commander of the battalion.[191] But they also helped Border Patrol agents stationed in Naco and Douglas by keeping an eye out for suspicious activities that might indicate drug trafficking or immigrants trying to enter the United States illegally.[192]

Prohibited from actually stopping, searching, or arresting subjects themselves, military troops, like the marines stationed outside Naco, stay in radio contact with civilian enforcement agencies. If the troops run into someone doing something they suspect is illegal, they summon the Border Patrol. In addition, Border Patrol agents and other law enforcement officers often accompany the troops in the field to supervise the operations, make arrests, and receive or provide training. When a small force of marines patrolling the Arizona border near Nogales in 1989 discovered a group of drug smugglers, for instance, the Border Patrol agent with the Marines authorized the troops to exchange fire with the traffickers.[193]

Operations like these are becoming more common along the border. In fact, military spokespersons acknowledge that ten such operations probably take place at any given time. A spokesperson for JTF-6 told a reporter investigating the maneuvers around Naco in August 1992 that there were sixty-two joint military-civilian exercises occurring at the time.[194] Cooperative exercises aimed at border control have occurred simultaneously along the border in all four border states.[195]

The campaign to integrate and coordinate activities, resources, and strategies among military and civilian agencies has been far-reaching but not always successful.[196] Illegal immigration and narcotrafficking continue at high levels, and many border residents express concern that the borderlands have become a virtual war zone. In fact, that is exactly what Border Patrol agents and military troops often call the most highly trafficked sections of the boundary.

Joint operations between the border police and the military have steadily become more technologically sophisticated. At five sites along the border immense aerostat radar balloons patrol the airspace. Although there are many difficulties with them—they have to be taken down in bad weather, they cannot "see" over hills or in canyons, and they require frequent maintenance—they contribute to the image of a militarized border. For Operation Alliance, the Department of Defense has contributed Blackhawk helicopters, high-speed interceptor planes, and radar planes, including an AWACS. Military troops have flown intrusion detection missions designed to monitor air traffic into the United States that may be involved with drug running. From the Department of Defense the INS has obtained A-Star 350 helicopters outfitted with powerful Nite Sun searchlights and infrared radar to track smugglers and undocumented immigrants entering the United States at night.

In one case the marines deployed a drone (a small, remotely piloted aircraft) equipped with high-tech observational equipment. It flew along the Texas-Mexico border for a couple of weeks, transmitting its observations to U.S. Marine monitors. They passed along the information to the Border Patrol, which used the tips to locate and seize several large marijuana shipments and to pick up double the number of undocumented immigrants usually captured during the same time period.

The National Guard tends to provide most of the labor and muscle for these operations, inspecting cargo at border crossings, building roads, cleaning ditches, and repairing fences, for instance. But it, too, increasingly relies on various types of high-tech equipment. Forward-looking infrared radar, side-looking airborne radar, and secure voice radio communications support

National Guard troops who carry out photo reconnaissance missions or other technical border-control activities. Likewise, the Border Patrol has enhanced its arsenal of detection devices. On the ground, its agents and their military colleagues employ sensitive detection devices that use seismic vibrations or infrared to pick up movement that may mean undocumented immigrants or traffickers are trying to cross the border. Outfitted with night scopes, night vision goggles, tripod-and vehicle-mounted scopes, they monitor high-traffic areas. They even monitor some stretches of the border with low-light closed-circuit television systems.

Critics of these types of programs fear the erosion of human and civil rights in the borderlands. Because military troops are trained to kill, not to make careful legal distinctions, they are dangerous additions to law-enforcement efforts. Along with efforts during the 1980s to devise "contingency plans" for border civil control and roundup of unwanted populations, these operations at their worst could provide the framework for police-state intervention like that seen during the Los Angeles riots in 1992.[197] During those riots Border Patrol agents were dispatched to Latino immigrant communities, where they picked up a thousand undocumented people and dispatched them to the INS for deportation.[198]

Even without going that far, the effect on the human and civil rights of people who look "foreign" has already been negative. Civilian law-enforcement agencies like the Border Patrol, Drug Enforcement Administration, customs, and state and local police forces are increasingly cross-designating (deputizing) personnel from other agencies, giving such agents broad authority over a range of jurisdictions. Through cross-designations, such agencies take on the role of a national police force. If "deputized" by customs, for example, agents can conduct warrantless searches if they suspect that someone is entering the United States illegally or with contraband.

Because civil rights violations like these are becoming more common and because the use of force—even deadly force—is occurring more frequently, a law professor at the University of Arizona described the borderlands as a "deconstitutionalized zone."[199] Roberto Martínez, director of the American Friends Service Committee's San Diego office, told a congressional committee: "As long as a segment of this society and government continues to lump together undocumented immigrants, drugs, crime, and terrorism to justify increased enforcement and militarization, attitudes toward immigrants will not only not change but will continue translating into open hostility and violence."[200]

Manufacturing on the Margin

Border business has long been regarded as a fringe economy. one that has little to do with the overall binational economic relations between Mexico and the United States.[201] Because of changing patterns of trade and investment and the rise of the Sun Belt, the perception of the marginal character of the border economy needs some updating.

Increasingly business along the international boundary line represents the shape of things to come throughout the United States and Mexico. Goods once available only in border stores are now available in supermarkets far outside the borderlands. Investment once restricted to Mexico's northern border is penetrating the interior. Like the border communities, the rest of the United States is awakening to challenges of global production sharing. Instead of hosting entire industries, the goal now is to hold on to supply businesses and the high-skill end of production. The informal service sector of Mexican maids and child care providers is emerging in cities far removed from the international border.

Free trade—and investment—are nothing new to the borderlands, but they are now coming as a shock to the rest of Mexico and the United States. "It's a new phenomenon for Washington and Mexico, but not for us," observed Elsa Saxod, San Diego's binational affairs director. "The industrial world and the developing world are coming together here on the border."[202]

When the line was drawn between Mexico and the United States in the mid-1800s, it gave rise to a new economy that fed on the differences between the two countries. In many cases, contraband dealings originally gave life to the border towns, in both Mexico and the United States. Although the vice business still exists, it has devolved into a minor sideline of the greater border economy. Trade liberalization has reduced the incentives for the trade in contraband consumer goods, with the exception of narcotrafficking, which has assumed a central, although clandestine, place in many border towns.

Investment and trade along the border have carved their own distinctive patterns. Especially for the Mexican border region, but also for the United States, these economic relations have pulled the two border economies closer together. The Mexican government has launched numerous programs designed to draw the borderlands closer to the national center, while the U.S. government has until recently mostly ignored the special economic problems of its southern border.

For Mexico, the northern border region has long been regulated by radically different economic policies from the rest of the country. The government's export-oriented development policies for the northern borderlands have been the prominent exception to Mexico's long history of import-substituting industrialization, protectionism, and nationalistic investment regulations. Since the late 1850s border states have at various time established free zones along the border to increase the ability of Mexican retailers to compete with their U.S. competitors. In 1965 the Mexican government opened its northern border to export-processing U.S. investment through its Border Industrialization Program, an initiative that stood in stark contrast to the domestic focus of its national economic policy. On the one hand, the Mexican government encouraged U.S. companies to move to the borderlands and set up maquiladoras (assembly plants), while on the other, it discouraged foreign investment in the country's interior with its "Mexicanization" policies.

The Border Industrialization Program was Mexico's first major departure from its strategy of restricting foreign investment and reducing dependence on the international economy. This program waived a number of foreign investment restrictions and import rules for export-oriented assembly plants. With few exceptions, plants set up under this program, called maquiladoras, could be 100 percent foreign-owned.[203] Initially they had to be located within 12.5 miles of the border, but in 1972 the Echeverría administration eliminated this restriction, prohibiting maquilas only in Mexico's three largest cities: the capital, Guadalajara, and Monterrey.[204]

Originally seen as a gimmick to provide employment to returning *braceros*, the maquila program had by the mid-1980s become a "priority sector" for Mexico, according to President de la Madrid.[205] By the early 1990s export-oriented industrialization and the production-sharing model of the maquilas were central to the Salinas administration's development strategy for Mexico.[206]

The Border Industrialization Program represented the first step towards the integration of Mexico into the U.S. manufacturing base. But regional integration was hardly what Mexico had in mind in establishing the program. Until the mid-1980s the country's economic planners viewed it largely as an employment program. Although employee training is an additional potential benefit, most jobs are unskilled, and many positions in engineering and management (with the exception of personnel administration) are held by foreigners.

Along with allowing full foreign ownership, the most attractive aspect of the Border Industrialization Program for foreign manufacturers was the exemption from duties of all imported inputs—materials, components, machinery, and tools. To qualify for these exemptions, a firm was required to ship all waste and scrap by products out of the country along with the finished product and had to post a bond for the value of the duties that were waived. This latter requirement led to the phrase in-bond assembly operations, which is used interchangeably with maquiladoras and maquilas.

By any name the program has changed the face of Mexico's northern border region. Industrial parks have sprouted up from Tijuana to Matamoros, and around them maquila workers and other impoverished border residents have constructed shanty-towns of makeshift huts. Maquila operations span a very wide range of activities, from the assembly of plastic toys and polyester lingerie to the highly complex management of a modern lumber mill. At eight maquiladoras owned by the A.C. Nielsen company, workers sort millions of coupons for U.S. manufacturers and retailers. Catalina Offshore Products sends U.S. sea urchins to its maquiladora in Ensenada for processing into sushi. At the Allen Coach Works plant in Nuevo Laredo, workers saw Cadillacs and Lincoln Continentals in half and then refashion the luxury cars into limousines.

Despite the shift from a regional to a national development program, the maquila sector remains concentrated on the northern border. It is here where foreign investors find the combination of cheap labor, proximity to U.S. markets and suppliers, and infrastructure that best enhances their competitive advantage. About 80 percent of the assembly plants are still found along Mexico's northern border, mostly in the major cities of Juárez, Tijuana, Nogales, Mexicali, Matamoros, Reynosa, and Nuevo Laredo.[207] In search of still cheaper labor, some firms have established plants as far away from the border as the Yucatán and Oaxaca, while others looking for an untapped skilled-labor market have set up maquilas in such places as Chihuahua, Hermosillo, and the outskirts of Guadalajara. But proximity to U.S. suppliers and the U.S. market ensures that the border is likely to remain the premier location for export-processing industries, even after a U.S.-Mexico free trade accord.

From Screwdrivers to Robots

Maquila trade—imported inputs to Mexico and exported assembled goods to the United States—constitutes one-third of the two-way trade between the two nations. Economic changes and aggressive promotion have prompted rapid growth in the maquiladora program. The number of assembly plants jumped from 585 in 1982 to 1,125 in 1987, and passed 2,000 in 1992. The number of employees grew even faster, because of the increasing size of the average plant's work force.

Not only have the numbers of factories and workers increased since the 1960s, but the types of industries setting up maquiladoras have also dramatically changed. No longer do low-tech or so-called screwdriver industries dominate the maquila sector. Instead, electronics and auto-parts plants that increasingly feature high-tech production systems are the leading industries—together accounting for about half the maquila work force and value-added production. Automatic insertion machines and surface-mount technology were added to circuit board assembly lines, clean rooms to the semiconductor industry, and robots to metal machining processes. Value added per employee—one indication of the technological level of a process—increased from $5,780 in 1983 to $7,794 in 1989.[208] As Ford's engine plant in Chihuahua and dozens of other state-of-the-art Mexican facilities demonstrate, Mexican workers are quite capable of turning out high-quality, high-technology products.

Border towns such as Juárez and Mexicali have become high-tech centers for leading defense and aeronautical corporations such as Hughes Aircraft, TRW, Rockwell, McDonnell Douglas, and

Bell and Howell. Auditors and quality-control agents from the Defense Contract Administration Services regularly cross the border to monitor the military-related manufacturing in the maquila plants.

Jobs, Jobs, Jobs

On a certain level the success of the Border Industrialization Program is beyond dispute. The economic boom of Mexico's northern cities is largely attributable to the maquiladoras, and U.S. border cities also have benefited from an associated service industry and a healthy commercial sector fueled by the maquila boom and population growth. Although it is not hard to find critics of the pay levels and the environmental repercussions of the maquila industry, most borderlanders or *fronterizos* support the presence of the maquila industry. Especially in Mexico, they recognize it as a major source of jobs.

As an employment-generating strategy, the Border Industrialization Program has certainly worked. Unemployment in most Mexican border cities is minimal, especially when compared with elsewhere in Mexico. From around 20,000 employees in 1970, maquila employment grew to nearly 130,000 in 1980 and to more than 500,000 by the end of 1992. A recent survey in Nogales, Sonora found that 45 percent of the work force in that Mexican city was directly or indirectly tied to the maquila industry.[209]

Mexico's net income from the program, the vast majority of which corresponds to workers' wages, replaced tourism as the country's second largest source of foreign exchange in the late 1980s. In 1992 nearly five billion dollars flowed to Mexico's central bank as maquila owners traded dollars for pesos to pay their workers and other costs in Mexico.[210] Only oil exports, worth almost eight billion dollars in 1992, earned more foreign currency. Direct investment in maquiladora plants and equipment brings in another few hundred million dollars in an average year.[211]

The maquiladoras have incorporated more sophisticated technology and higher value-added activity into their assembly systems, but wages are still extremely low (about sixty dollars per forty-five-hour week) despite increasing productivity.[212] The low wage rates caused by the devaluation of the Mexican peso sparked the maquila boom of the 1980s. These wages, lower than those paid in other leading export-processing centers and lower than those paid by Mexican manufacturers, are not nearly enough to provide for a family, and they keep maquila workers living in makeshift homes in squatter colonies that often lack water and sewage services.[213]

Rather than attempt to reduce high turnover rates and to increase worker productivity by offering higher wages, the maquiladora managers entice workers with such perks as free lunches, beauty contests, company transportation, showers at work, and company-sponsored sports. Rather than raise wages, an article in *Twin Plant News* advised maquila managers: "There are some things you can do to help, such as setting up a clothing exchange in the plant. . . . Buy some bulk food items such as flour, beans, potatoes, etc., and distribute these among your employees."[214]

Maquila associations in every important city share information about their members' wage structure. The wage reports serve as guidelines and help ensure that companies do not enter a bidding war for the available labor force. Although the associations deny that their intention is to hold down wages, numerous investigators have found that maquila managers feel great pressure from their peers to maintain wages within a certain range.[215] The government aids employers in this endeavor, according to managers of two U.S.-owned auto plants. "We even get help from the government making sure that we don't settle too high" in negotiations with the union, said one. "The labor ministry takes an active part in negotiations, especially in companies our size. And they steer the level of increases," confirmed another.[216]

Extremely low wages produce high employee turnover in the maquiladoras as workers jump at any opportunity to earn more money. It is common for plants to lose one-tenth of their entire work forces in some months and to see more employees quit in one year than are employed at any given time.

Although some employers complain that such turnover costs them a significant amount of money—because of the constant need to retrain new workers—for most maquiladoras turnover is at worst a minor annoyance, and sometimes even helpful. Only a handful of maquiladoras provide more than a day or two of training for their assembly-line positions—where pay is lowest and turnover highest—and for many training lasts only a few hours.[217] In those plants that do provide greater training, it is generally provided only to workers with a minimum level of seniority—usually at least three months. Since most turnover occurs before this cutoff point, few workers with significant amounts of training actually leave their jobs.

Enclave Industrialization

Much as it had during the dictatorship of General Porfirio Díaz (1876-1911), foreign investment in the maquiladoras has created an enclave economy. It is an economy geographically located within Mexico but largely dependent on decisions made by corporate executives, consumers, and policy makers in the United States, and it generates few benefits for that part of society outside the enclave.

A major failure of the Border Industrialization Program has been its inability to spur the creation of linkages with the rest of the Mexican economy. This means that few Mexican industries, either along the border or elsewhere in Mexico, supply the maquiladoras. Neither do many Mexican businesses buy maquila-manufactured goods to be used as part of their own production process. Consequently, the beneficial impact in northern Mexico of the maquila sector is largely limited to job creation and the economic activity generated by worker spending.[218]

The logic of the maquiladora program, which relies on minimal government interference in corporate decisions to encourage foreign investment, has stifled efforts to extend its benefits beyond the creation of jobs. Mexican attempts to build linkages between the maquiladoras and the rest of the economy—through supply contracts or technology transfer, for example—have failed. Throughout the program the proportion of the value of production in maquiladoras that comes from Mexican-owned businesses has been under 2 percent.[219]

Because of its export orientation and its lack of linkages with the domestic economy, the maquila industry can be fairly described as a foreign-owned enclave economy. But the maquilas do not operate independently of the government and local capitalists. From the beginning of the Border Industrialization Program, a close partnership has developed among the Mexican state bureaucracy, the domestic economic elite, and the transnational corporations that operate the maquilas.[220] Not only has the government financed construction of numerous industrial parks, but it has also supported the maquilas by providing land, roads, and public utilities—and by leaving them virtually untaxed and unregulated.

By keeping a tight lid on independent union activity and by having government-affiliated labor confederations work closely with the maquila management, the Mexican government has also sided with the interests of the maquila sector to the detriment of Mexican workers.[221] In the mid-1970s, when labor organizing was threatening to drive wages up, the government and the maquila industry even entered into an "Alliance for Production."[222] Shortly thereafter the Confederation of Mexican Workers (CTM), the official labor union, regained control of the plants, independent organizing was suppressed, and the peso was devalued, all of which made Mexico once again a desirable offshore location for production-sharing industries. So compatible are the industry and official unions that many corporations actually favor having a union to reduce the turnover rate and increase productivity.[223]

Like the government, Mexican capitalists and professionals play an important role in making the maquila sector work smoothly. Their most important role is facilitating maquila operations by managing industrial parks, providing legal and accounting services, arranging transportation, and serving as customs brokers.[224] In each of the main border cities, a local bourgeoisie feeds off of the maquila sector.[225] According to one estimate, the Mexican companies that run the industrial parks can clear as much as fifty cents an hour per maquila employee.[226] The most powerful of these firms is Grupo Bermúdez of Juárez, founded by Antonio Bermúdez, the same man who ran the government's nationalist PRONAF (National Border Program) campaign in the early 1960s.[227]

Whereas the Mexican government has gone to great lengths to assist the maquila industry and shelter it from labor and environmental regulations, it has largely ignored the basic needs of its work force. The small amount of revenue collected from the maquiladoras goes not to local governments but to the national treasury, leaving Mexican border towns no funds to cope with immense public health and housing problems.

Although central to the economy of the Mexican borderlands, maquila-based development has accentuated the planning and infrastructural problems faced by Mexican cities. Most obvious are the housing crisis and the lack of waste disposal and wastewater treatment facilities. Electricity, water, and roads were extended to the maquiladoras; but little thought was given to the social and environmental costs of the maquila boom. So grave are some of these problems that Juárez at one point even began to discourage new maquila growth. At a time when growing environmental consciousness, high labor turnover, and urban congestion are making the border region less desirable, some companies are discovering the advantages of establishing maquiladoras deeper in Mexico. New communications and transportation networks will make nonborder locations increasingly attractive, especially considering the still lower labor costs of most nonborder sites.

The Border Industrialization Program has accomplished its chief objectives of generating employment for the border region and increasing the inflow of foreign exchange. But it has failed to build a foundation for the broad-based economic development of northern Mexico. After more than twenty-five years the maquila sector remains an assembly-manufacturing enclave controlled by transnational corporations. The Mexican government now hopes that the maquilas can serve as a model for export-oriented industrialization along the lines experienced by Taiwan, South Korea, Singapore, and Hong Kong. Unlike the Asian tigers, however, Mexico has failed to use the maquila sector as a stepping-stone to full-fledged industrialization.[228]

Recent trade and investment liberalization initiatives on the part of the Mexican government show no sign of sparking more integral development. Thus far there is nothing to indicate that Mexico will be able to foster more meaningful technology transfer or increase the economic linkages outside the foreign-owned enclave.[229] In the absence of local-content regulations and an active government role in linking suppliers with exporters, companies have little incentive to seek out local firms and work with them to improve quality and reliability.

What few inputs come from the borderlands region are generally supplied not by Mexican companies but by firms on the U.S. side, especially in Texas and Southern California.[230] In the absence of foreign-investment regulations that require more linkages with the national economy if willing and able suppliers are available, it makes more sense for companies to look to U.S. suppliers for the inputs they need. At this point companies have little incentive to seek out local suppliers in the Mexican interior unless quality can be guaranteed and there exist real price advantages.

The most fervent proponents of export-processing industrialization assert that Mexico is poised for an economic takeoff similar to that experienced by the Asian tigers more than two decades ago. But a visit to any one of the maquila zones that hug the border gives a more sobering picture of Mexico's prospects for using maquila production as a base for broader economic development. Hundreds of workers in Nogales, Sonora, produce automatic garage door openers for Sears at a massive warehouse-style factory, and many live in hovels of their own making just outside the high barbed wire fence surrounding the plant. Like many other maquila workers, their homes are worth less than the products they assemble every day. Can economic growth and prosperity be the product of such misery?

Economic growth, meaning the expansion of the gross domestic product (GDP), can result from minimum-wage manufacturing. But making export-processing zones into development zones is a challenge that Mexico has not met after more than a quarter-century of hosting maquilas. No matter how many maquilas come to the border, or anywhere else in Mexico, it appears likely that development will not follow unless the Mexican government aggressively promotes more linkages with domestic producers, genuine technology transfer, and better wages and conditions for the maquila work force. In addition, as is becoming increasingly obvious, economic growth—whether through maquila manufacturing or domestic industrialization—will actually subvert development unless it is environmentally sustainable and its costs and benefits are fairly distributed.

The problems of environmental destruction, inadequate social infrastructure, and the exploitation of the country's work force are, of course, not attributable solely to the maquilas or the government's export-oriented development strategy. Rather they are symptoms of Mexico's failure to shape economic policies that ensure that the benefits of economic development are broadly shared.

The expectation in the Mexican borderlands is that expanded economic integration—as represented most dramatically by the prospect of free trade—will mean more investment and jobs for the region. Furthermore, many predict that the advance of production-sharing and flexible production strategies will result in the increased flow of high-tech industry to the northern border states. However, to ensure that this projected flow of investment, technology, and jobs nurtures broad-based and sustained development, the Mexican government will need to assume more control over the nature and direction of export-oriented manufacturing—a challenge that will be increasingly difficult within the context of a free trade agreement.

The danger, as industry spokespeople are fond of repeating, is that government regulation, such as increased minimum wages or mandatory local-supply requirements, will "kill the goose that lays the golden eggs." This is the same implied threat, of course, that industries are using against the U.S. government and U.S. workers. Throughout the Mexican borderlands, there exists a deep awareness about how dependent the regional economy is on the maquila industry. Although few borderlanders outside of the maquila business sector would describe the eggs laid by the maquilas as golden, a future without these assembly plants looks even more bleak than the present borderland reality.

As many maquila workers are well aware, their wages are low—but not as low as those being paid in places such as Haiti and Malaysia or, for that matter, by the maquila sector farther south in their own country. Although companies publicly talk of relocation to lower-wage locations mainly as an idle threat to keep wages low and the government cooperative, some maquilas have indeed closed down and moved to Southeast Asia.[231] Increasingly, the structure and the mobility of global production limit the development choices open to Mexico and its borderlands.

Whither the Maquiladoras under Free Trade?

Talk of free trade raised questions about the future of the maquila sector. At the very least Mexico would have to revamp the legal framework of the Border Industrialization Program. Since the ability to import parts duty-free into Mexico from the United States would no longer remain unique to maquiladoras there would be no need for in-bond treatment of those imports. In addition, requiring certain manufacturers to export their production would become meaningless when those exports could reenter Mexico duty-free.[232]

The NAFTA text signed in late 1992 required Mexico to phase out the maquiladora program over the course of seven years. But few, if any, of the maquiladoras themselves would be forced out of business by the pact. Many maquila managers had feared that their reliance on Asian components would disqualify their products for duty-free status under NAFTA. The amounts in question are not small. Roughly 45 percent of all maquila inputs have traditionally originated outside the United States and Mexico. In the end, though, negotiators adopted a loose rule of origin, as it is called, for most industries. To qualify for duty-free status, a product that came into North America under one tariff heading had only to be transformed sufficiently within the continent to be classified under a different tariff heading. Even if no tariff classification change occurred, up to 40 percent of the value of a product was allowed to originate outside the North American region without invalidating that product's duty-free status. These rules posed little threat to most maquiladoras.

Of greater importance to maquila operators were the special restrictions tacked on to a number of the sector's most prominent products: auto parts, televisions, computers, and textiles. As a result of strong lobbying efforts by politically powerful U.S. industries, producers of these goods will either have to meet higher regional content requirements or incorporate specific regionally produced components to gain duty-free status.[233]

Although these special restrictions demonstrate that NAFTA—like all regional free trade agreements—is as much about managing trade as freeing it, they are unlikely to cause many maquiladoras to close shop. Most producers who do not currently meet the regional-content rules will be able to shift sources of supply relatively quickly. After analyzing NAFTA's provisions, one major economics forecasting firm predicted the maquiladora industry would grow by an average annual rate of 8.5 percent from 1993 to 1997.[234]

With the tariff reduction that free trade would bring, the incentive to use U.S. components and raw materials would drop. Maquilas might find it advantageous to find suppliers within Mexico for such items as varied as cardboard packaging and plastics-injection molding. There is also some concern in the U.S. borderlands that to the extent that dependence on imported inputs diminishes, so do incentives to locate near the border. Instead of proximity to the United States, manufacturers may begin to place a higher value on the abundance of manual labor, the availability of local inputs, and the presence of economic infrastructure.[235] But given that the major market for the assembled goods will still be the United States, proximity to the border will remain an important factor. And although the infrastructure of the Mexican borderlands is inadequate, it is for the most part still superior to that found elsewhere in Mexico as is the ability of local industry to supply inputs.

Having paved the way for U.S.-Mexico integration and having set the tone for Mexico's economic development strategy, the labor-intensive assembly plants are here to stay even if the maquiladora program is phased out. But residents of the borderlands are ambivalent about free trade and further economic integration. The prospect of new manufacturing investment, higher levels of trade, and increased cross-border retailing has raised hopes in the region. But the failed promises of the past and the likely costs of economic growth cast some doubt on claims that the benefits of any rise in cross-border trade and investments will be widespread.

Chapter *7*

Dual Development: The Neverending Promise

In its early days the Border Industrialization Program was promoted on the U.S. side as the Twin Plant Program. The idea was that for every maquiladora on the Mexican side there would be another plant on the U.S. side of the border in charge of supply and final assembly. But this promise was never realized. Companies did open offices and warehouses on the U.S. side, but only rarely were actual manufacturing operations established in the U.S. twin city. Customs regulations requiring that assembled manufactures crossing the border be "finished" in the United States have been largely ignored. Sticking a "Made in the U.S.A." sticker on the maquila products or warehousing them on the U.S. side are often the only "finishing" operations done in the United States.

What has mainly emerged along the U.S. border are service industries to support the Mexican factories with transportation, communications, financing, warehousing, and some intermediate (mainly packaging) and capital-intensive supplies. The owners of these service and supply industries became the strongest backers of the maquila-centered model of economic growth on the U.S. side of the border. Despite the inaccuracy of the term, it is still used by groups like the Twin Plant Wives Association and the *Twin Plant News* to propagate the idea that maquiladoras foster substantial economic growth in the U.S. borderlands.

In 1990 the mayor of El Paso proclaimed the city the "Maquila Capital of the World," kicking off a week of events promoting the maquila industry that was organized by members of the local Twin Plants Wives Association. There are no maquiladoras in El Paso and only a few of what could be described as twin plants. Nonetheless, El Paso considers itself the maquila capital because Juárez is the twin city with the largest maquila work force.

For most U.S. border towns, the economic development strategies of town leaders have been closely linked to attracting businesses from the Rust Belt to the Sun Belt. The sunnier climate of the borderlands—including the possibility of "playing golf year-round," as most development brochures point out—is always part of the sales pitch. But knowing that corporations do not make siting decisions on the sunshine factor alone, the industrial development organizations get quickly to the main sales pitch: "the abundant labor at low, low cost" of the U.S. and Mexican borderlands.[236]

The border towns are, of course, not the only communities that have based their economic development on the attraction of corporations with assurances of low wages, no unions, government subsidies, tax incentives, and sometimes even free land. For the past three decades this type of strategy has been common throughout the South and the Southwest. Seeing their industries run away to the South, towns in the Midwest and Northeast in the 1980s also frantically began to match the kinds of incentives advertised by the southern states while workers offered voluntarily to reduce wages and benefits if companies would stay in town.

What has made the industrial development strategy of the U.S. border communities so distinctive is that they search out companies to move not to their own home towns but primarily to their twin cities in Mexico. The low wages of El Paso do contrast sharply with industrial wage rates farther north, but the city's economic planners have concluded that El Paso's main attraction is its proximity to Mexico. The main benefit to El Paso—and other border cities, such as Brownsville, that rely on similar development strategies—is not a large increase in the employment base. Instead, the payoff is more service business (banking, warehousing, transportation, etc.) and to a lesser extent a small supply sector and the retail trade (as maquila workers spend their paychecks) generated by the new maquiladoras.

In pursuit of this maquila-based development, the El Paso Industrial Development Corporation, which counts on substantial annual contributions from the city treasury, has sent its representatives out to the Rust Belt in search of runaway industries. While wining and dining prospectives, they try to lure them south with tales of ten-dollar-a-day workers, no unions, and golf in December. For the most part, however, the border cities rely on business-magazine advertising. "We Introduce the Movers to the

Shakers" is the come-on used by an advertisement placed by the El Paso Industrial Development Corporation in the *Twin Plant News*. In the early 1990s the group began trying to shake some of the defense industries loose from California and persuade them to move El Paso or to Juárez, the Mexican city that is already the location of several firms producing for military contracts including Westinghouse and General Electric.[237]

Maquiladora Colleges

Joining the city managers and business establishment, the post-secondary institutions of the borderlands are also playing a part in fostering the expansion and development of the maquila sector.[238] With the belief that what is good for the maquila sector is good for U.S. border communities, area colleges are training both U.S. and Mexican students to meet the employment needs of the maquilas. Recognizing the rising demand for high-tech services, some of these institutions also serve the maquilas by facilitating the incorporation of high-tech operations into their local assembly process.

Community colleges along the border—from the Texas Southmost College in Brownsville to Southwestern Community College in Chula Vista, California—have introduced courses specifically designed to train maquila technicians, direct-line supervisors, and managers. An article in *Twin Plant News* aptly called the community colleges along the border the "Maquiladora Colleges."[239] At its International Trade Center, Southwestern Community College offers courses that instruct students in the legal aspects and labor-management problems of the maquila industry. Texas Southmost College, like many of the region's community colleges, offers courses in customized manufacturing processes tailored to specific plants in Mexico.

The federally supported Advanced Technology Center (ATC) at the El Paso Community College goes a step further, directly contracting with the maquiladoras to offer technology transfer and training courses to the management and work force—all done in Spanish and at the company's plant in Mexico. The ATC's director Mike Roark explained that ATC was founded to "meet the expanding maquila industry's need for specialized skills" but noted that it provides customized training only for 100 percent U.S.-owned maquilas, not for joint ventures with Mexicans or foreign-owned maquilas.[240] When ATC promotional brochures state that its mission is to "promote economic development" and respond to the needs of "local industry," by *local* they mean not only El Paso but also Juárez.

Besides offering customized training in plastics injection techniques and other technologies to meet the needs of companies like General Motors' Delco-Remy division, the El Paso Community College also works closely with Mexico's National College of Professional Technical Education (CONALEP) in a plastics injection training project sponsored by the Grupo Bermúdez maquila promoters. "We're training them to train their own people," said Roark.[241] Working closely with the Maquila Association in Juárez, CONALEP is expanding its support role to the maquilas, including the construction of a new facility built in a Juárez industrial park that will train people in plastic-injection molding, computer technology, and other skills needed by the maquiladoras.[242] The ATC also trains operators for the sizable plastic-injection industry in El Paso, but one wonders how long this and other high-tech service industries will remain on the U.S. side.

This partnership between academia and industry is still more pronounced at the University of Texas. In Brownsville, the Pan American campus has a Center for Entrepreneurship and Economic Development, which provides technical assistance to firms starting or expanding maquiladoras. The University of Texas at El Paso (UTEP) is continuing its long history as an industry school (it was founded in 1914 as the School of Mines and Metallurgy). The difference is that the industry it is now serving is found increasingly in Mexico.

The university is a top player in turning the maquila sector into a high-tech industry. With the help of university staff, the maquiladoras are incorporating such technologies as robotics, computer vision, and real-time process control into the assembly process. The center of support services for the maquila industry at UTEP is the Institute for Manufacturing and Materials Management (IM³), which depends on federal and state funds as well as private contracts. Asked about the propriety of using government and university funds to assist maquila production, IM³'s Erin Ross replied, "I feel we are subsidizing the American economy and the American companies, which make American profits and pay American taxes."[243]

Founded by and closely associated with IM[3] is the Machine Vision Applications Laboratory (MVAL), which serves such firms as Ford, General Motors, and Honeywell in Juárez to help them apply advanced technologies and techniques to their manufacturing processes. Partnership between academia and business is built into the MVAL. Kenneth Chapman helped establish the machine-vision technology application program, which provides automated quality-control processes, while on leave from Intelledex, a leading machine-vision equipment manufacturing company. At Ford's Coclisa air-conditioning assembly plant, MVAL installed a machine-vision computer system to inspect the quality of the finished parts after they concluded that "operator fatigue" was the main reason for faulty assembly.

Any remaining illusion that the maquila sector relies solely on low-technology production is quickly dispelled at such institutions as IM[3], ATC, or MVAL, all of which promote the idea that the maquilas should use "World-Class Manufacturing" techniques. As MVAL's Chapman advises, "These new technologies such as machine vision and robotics, coupled with quality-control techniques, such as statistical process control (SPC), kan-ban, just-in-time (JIT), and Poke-a-yoke, provide a path for continuous improvement and increased ability to compete effectively."[244] While this may well be true, critics of the economic development strategy embraced by most border cities believe that U.S. citizens are losing out when tax dollars are used to underwrite technology transfer programs that aid such companies as Delco-Remy, Honeywell, and Ford that closed down plants in the United States to open up their Juárez maquilas.[245] The promotion of high-tech production in Mexico also belies the claims of free marketers that U.S.-Mexico production sharing merely transfers undesirable low-tech operations to a low-wage country. But the real question facing border planners is to what extent industrial development in Mexico— either the low- or high-tech variety—contributes to economic growth and prosperity on the U.S. side.

The Vision of Dr. Michie

Besides directly serving the maquila industry, IM[3] is one of the borderlands' leading promoters of the maquila-centered strategy of economic development. Donald Michie, often described as IM[3]'s "mastermind," has probably been the region's leading spokesperson for the concept that the future of the borderlands are linked to maquila growth.

Before founding IM³, Michie served on the faculty of UTEP's business school and worked closely with the maquila industry and industrial promotional groups to prove that maquilas directly benefit U.S. border communities. In the mid-1980s, with Michie serving on its board, the El Paso Foreign Trade Association, an organization of those servicing and promoting the maquila sector, together with the El Paso Industrial Development Council and Juárez Economic Development commissioned a Project Link study by a researcher at UTEP's business school to demonstrate the links between maquilas and job creation in El Paso. The Project Link report concluded that one of every five new jobs in El Paso was linked to maquila growth in Juárez between 1976 and 1985.[246]

Although the study has been discredited because of its faulty methodology—not including job losses caused by maquilas, for example—Project Link's findings have been widely used by Michie and other maquila promoters such as the Border Trade Alliance to demonstrate that maquilas are good not only for Mexico but also for the U.S. border region.[247] Project Link continued the border tradition of having business-sponsored research support contentions by the maquila sector and its U.S. facilitators that maquilas boosted the U.S. economy and employment. Much of the early self-promotional research was sponsored by Grupo Bermúdez, the Juárez firm that is the region's largest operator of industrial parks.

In the early 1970s Grupo Bermúdez hired ex-U.S. army officer William Mitchell to search out U.S. corporations and persuade them to move to Mexico. Besides being enormously successful in this effort, Mitchell compiled "economic surveys" that purported to show how many U.S. jobs depended on maquila operations. This type of unabashed promotion of the maquila sector was continued in the 1980s by UTEP's Michie. Besides his association with Project Link, Michie also worked closely with the El Paso Foreign Trade Association and the Border Trade Alliance in producing its *Maquiladora Impact Survey* in 1987. Extrapolating from the survey results, Michie and the Border Trade Alliance have made highly exaggerated claims about the number of U.S. companies and jobs the maquila industry supports. Like earlier studies, the survey made no attempt to balance job losses against job creation. Moreover, Michie and the Border Trade Alliance used the survey to show that many companies—and all their employees— have been sustained simply because a maquila may have purchased a part or two from them. Michie went so far as to imply that the survey indicated that three million U.S. jobs depended on border maquilas.[248]

The promotional research by UTEP's Michie has continued into the 1990s. As the head of IM³, Michie remains a chief proponent of border development strategies linked to the production-sharing operations of the maquila sector. Heavily backed by government and the private sector, this approach has come to dominate economic development planning in the region. Among the principal functions of IM³ are community outreach to support development and the supply of borderlands economic data and analysis to the region's association of governors.[249] With the advent of free trade with Mexico and rising government attention to the borderlands, IM³ has benefited from large infusions of government research and technology transfer grants.

A 1991 report by IM³ persisted in claims about the "dramatic economic impact" of the maquila industry on the El Paso area. Although figures showing the high job creation effect of the maquilas are still presented as valid estimations, Michie and IM³ have begun to stress the role of the U.S. borderlands in integrating "higher technology processes into production-sharing industries." This is also a prominent component of the business promotion activities of the El Paso Industrial Development Corporation.

According to IM³, "The ability of materials management to combine technology with a relatively inexpensive labor force lies at the heart of our region's competitive advantage in the global economy." Furthermore, "U.S.-owned companies operating in Mexico play an increasingly important role in maintaining this competitive advantage."[250] IM³ believes that the El Paso area's future development lies in supplying materials, services, and technology to the maquila sector. In many ways, this is exactly the same line of reasoning used by the leading promoters of NAFTA and other global trade accords. When assembly operations leave for Mexico or other third world nations, they argue, the U.S. economy benefits not only by keeping its corporations competitive but also by supplying the capital goods and supplies needed by the maquiladoras. By virtue of its border location, El Paso stands first in line to provide those services, say groups like IM[3]: "The U.S.-Mexico border has become the front door, not the back door, to U.S.-Mexico and global commerce."[251]

Although this development strategy has certainly worked for many maquila facilitators and such institutions as the Advanced Technology Center and IM[3]—which have been swimming in government grants and private contracts—its benefits to the entire population have been less clear. The propaganda bandied about by Michie, IM[3], and the Border Trade Alliance that the borderlands have benefited from a maquila-based development strategy based on the presence of twin plants and maquila supply and service firms does not square with the dismal economic state of most U.S. border cities. Nor does it take into consideration the manifold environmental, infrastructural, and public-health problems caused by unregulated industrial development in the borderlands. In 1975 El Paso's per capita income was 22 percent below the statewide average for Texas. It then dropped to about 35 percent under the average by 1990 even though the maquila sector in Juárez exploded in the 1980s. In the early 1990s personal income continued to drop steadily. On the other side of the border the manufacturing sector has boomed, but the sad state of the infrastructure and the desperate living conditions of maquila workers challenge claims that maquila manufacturing is promoting economic development. Economic growth in Mexico and increasing U.S.-Mexico trade have resulted in higher-than-average economic growth and job creation in El Paso. But wages in most sectors remain abysmally low

The updated high-skill services vision of border development is also problematic. Like the earlier version, it predicates U.S. border prosperity on the flourishing of low-wage industry in Mexico. But the plan to convert the U.S. borderlands into a center of higher technology and technology transfer may be based on an optimistic understanding of the globalization process. It is true that there may be an expanded role for a small sector of technology-transfer consultants and those U.S. high-tech industries still reluctant for whatever reason to leave U.S. soil. As the forces of globalization build momentum, U.S. firms are no longer simply relegating their labor-intensive and low-technology production to Mexico. They are also relocating high-technology and capital goods manufacturing south of the border. Furthermore, the high-tech systems such as plastics-injection molding that border cities like El Paso hoped to corner are now also available in Mexico. Indeed, taxpayer-supported centers like ATC and IM³ are among the ones facilitating the technology transfer process.

Promoting economic development in the borderlands is no easy task. Proximity to the abundant, low-wage labor supply in Mexico exerts downward pressure on wage rates on the U.S. side while a steady influx of immigrants keeps unemployment high. Strategies to attract low-wage, low-tech assembly industries to the U.S. borderlands have met with some success but numerous manufacturers have later decided to move all or part of their operations over to the Mexican side. Since 1986 El Paso has lost at least 2,750 manufacturing jobs as firms such as Farah, Billy the Kid, and Dale Electronics have relocated to Juárez and other Mexican border towns.[252] The city's economic development specialists have lately attempted to promote El Paso as a sourcing center for high-tech supplies and services. Although they have met with some success, particularly in the field of plastics-injection molding, this new twist of the earlier version of maquila-tied development has not supplied the quantity and quality of jobs that El Paso needs if it is to lower its unemployment rate and raise wage levels. There is also the latent threat that as the economic infrastructure and skill levels in Juárez and other border cities improve, these high-tech industries may also find it more economical to do business entirely in Mexico.

But officials of El Paso's development agencies are not worried. They feel that as the Mexican economy improves and industrialization expands, the benefits will boomerang back to El Paso in the form of increased retail trade and supply sourcing. But the question about whether the foundation for prosperity in the U.S. borderlands can be constructed from low-wage industrialization in Mexico remains. Border planners are faced with the challenge of raising educational levels, productivity, and wage rates while lowering unemployment at the same time as they offer tax abatements to industry, discourage unionization, and promote the region as a low-cost center.

Free Trading and Cross Shopping

With the Border Industrialization Program and the rise of the maquila economy, the international border became increasingly meaningless as a barrier to U.S. investment and production sharing. But long before the borderlands turned into an export-processing zone for foreign investors, cross-border shopping had made economic integration a daily reality.

In the mid-1800s a boundary line was drawn between the free wheeling capitalism of the U.S. frontier and the highly protectionist and highly taxed Mexican society.[253] Distance and the northern deserts isolated the Mexican interior from the lures and advances of U.S. traders, but the population of *el norte* was more vulnerable. In fact, it had little choice—given the expense, lack of variety, and poor quality of goods shipped from central Mexico—but to do its shopping on the U.S. side. In response to surveys showing that as much as two-thirds of border spending was going to U.S. retailers and wholesalers, in 1971 the federal government introduced the Artículos Ganchos or "hook items" program whereby Mexican consumers could buy certain U.S. manufactured goods from Mexican stores at the same prices available on the U.S. side. The main focus was to boost the sagging sales of Mexican retailers, but like other such free trade initiatives the program seemed only to spur more smuggling.

Cross-border shopping is the lifeblood of many U.S. border communities.[254] The downtown stores commonly rely on Mexican shoppers for 90 percent of their business, while, depending on the border town, 25 to 70 percent of the entire retail-trade business comes from Mexican buyers.[255] Although border merchants have depended on Mexican consumers, they have generally not provided them with any special services. Retailers reach out to Mexicans with electronic and newspaper advertising. Border newspapers, like the *El Paso Times*, have Spanish-language sections aimed at Mexican readers. Consumers from Juárez can be seen carrying the ad-packed *Vecinos* (Neighbors) along on shopping trips to El Paso. Advertising for U.S. brand-name jeans, athletic shoes, and other hot items attracts many Mexican consumers. But advertising hype explains only a small portion of the cross-border retail trade. Because of trade barriers, the lack of domestic production, and the absence of a large concentrated market, many manufactured goods are cheaper in the United

States and often of superior quality. In fact, many assume that anything made in the United States is superior to the counterpart Mexican product.

Before the 1976 and 1982 devaluations of the peso, it was commonly estimated that maquila employees were spending well over half their disposable income across the border. That percentage declined sharply immediately after the 1982 devaluation, although it later rose as the peso stabilized and inflationary pressures in Mexico intensified. Estimates of what percentage of maquila wages is spent in the United States still vary widely, but most agree that maquila workers now spend a considerably smaller portion of their wages across the border than they did before 1982. Earning about sixty-five dollars weekly, maquila workers live on a tight budget and have little money for cross-border shopping trips. A recent study of Juárez maquila line workers found that half spent nothing in El Paso and the rest spent less than ten dollars a week.[256] A similar survey in Nogales reported that maquila line workers were spending about a quarter of their wages on the U.S. side, although technicians and managers were spending considerably more.[257]

Most of the direct leakage from the maquila sector seems not to be coming from the maquila production workers but from salaried professionals whose numbers have been steadily increasing especially in high-tech sites like Juárez and Mexicali.[258] Generally, Mexican white-collar workers have cars and prefer shopping at the malls, department stores, and flea markets on the U.S. side, while blue-collar workers with little income and no personal transportation do considerably less cross-border shopping.[259] Of the money that maquila workers do spend in the United States, more than 70 percent goes to such basic items as clothes and food.[260]

Maquilas are only one factor supporting the border retail trade. The U.S. border cities attract consumers from throughout northern Mexico, especially from such large cities as Chihuahua and Monterrey that are within easy driving distance of the border. Also boosting retail sales in the U.S. borderlands are the purchases of the more than one million Mexican holders of work permits or daily crossing permits.

As merchants discovered in the 1976 and 1982 peso devaluations, their dependence on these Mexican consumers for such a large portion of their sales implies certain risks, because when the value of the peso drops in relation to the dollar, it means that U.S. goods are suddenly out of reach for most Mexican families. The downtown business districts, which capture most of the pedestrian traffic, are hardest hit, but the effect of a peso devaluation reverberates throughout the entire border economy.

For local government, it means less revenue from bridge and sales taxes. Real estate markets slump, bank deposits drop, and hotel rooms remain empty. Just as poor Mexicans were no longer able to buy their food and clothes on the U.S. side, wealthy Mexicans could no longer afford a condominium on South Padre Island (offshore of Brownsville). Cities without their own industrial bases, such as Brownsville and Laredo, suffer more than the diversified economies of El Paso and San Diego. Following the 1982 devaluation, employment dropped by 11 percent in Brownsville and by nearly 20 percent in Laredo because of reduced retail trade.[261]

By the mid-1980s the peso had stabilized and U.S. border towns began perking up again. Once again the streets of downtown El Paso and the malls of Laredo were filled with Mexican shoppers. In fact, retail chains such as Sam's reported having a higher retail value of sales per square meter of floor space than stores in much larger cities like New York or Dallas. At one shopping mall in Laredo, sales were double the national average for the twenty other malls owned by the company.[262] By 1990 Mexicans were spending as much money in the United States as they had in the boom year of 1979 before Mexico slid into *la crisis*.[263]

Retail sales picked up in all border towns, but the new boom was probably most evident in Nogales, Arizona. Border fences and customs checks keep Ambos Nogales physically divided, but family and shopping bring the two border communities together socially and economically. Those that do not have the proper permits slip through one of the many person-size holes cut in the border fence. On a typical Saturday morning hundreds of *nogalenses* without border-crossing cards become illegal aliens for a day as they scurry across the boundary to do their weekly shopping at Safeway and the department stores on the U.S. side. The Border Patrol usually does not bother these illegal shoppers, and certainly not when they are making their return trip to Mexico carting bags of U.S. goods.

Downtown Nogales has become a retail battle zone. Local realtors say that retail space on the two blocks of Morley Avenue is more expensive than on Central Avenue in Phoenix. Safeway is doing three times the business it was built to handle, and the Payless Shoe store in Nogales outsells all but a few of the 3,000 other branch outlets around the nation. As in other border cities, there is a distinct Asian-American flavor to this retail frenzy. Seizing the opportunity, Korean-American and Chinese-American entrepreneurs in the 1980s began opening up stores in the downtown districts of Nogales, El Paso, and other border cities.

Lumping all Asians together, Nogales locals call one shopping strip—which hosts Seoul II, Tienda De Lee, and Su's Kitchen—the Ho Chi Minh Trail.[264] Unlike the past, when the typical border merchant gouged Mexican consumers with high prices, the new wave of merchandisers wages war with one another to offer the lowest prices. Not only is the downtown district booming, but the whole town of Nogales is riding the crest of soaring retail and home sales.

Although most border business and government officials lined up behind NAFTA, the merchandising sector regards free trade with some trepidation. Even before the signing of the accord, re-tailing giants such as Price Club and Wal-Mart began moving across the border. As Mexico's program of trade and investment liberalization advances, U.S. wholesalers have begun to sell directly to large Mexican department stores such as Aurrera and Gigante while the larger U.S. retailing chains are deciding to open their own stores in Mexico. As more and more U.S. goods are available in stores on their own side, fewer Mexican consumers will see the need to cross the line to do their shopping. Mexicans will still be buying U.S. goods—and probably more of them—but their money will not be en-tering the economies of the border towns.

In anticipation of free trade, some border retailers are planning to relocate to Mexico while others will probably shut down. Overall the drop in border retail trade may be as high as 50 percent. The other great fear is that in the event of another large peso devaluation Mexican consumers will once again stay at home, setting off another wave of bankruptcies and layoffs across the U.S. borderlands. How-ever, with the increase of U.S. goods moving into Mexico, well-posi-tioned border businesses may find themselves ideally situated to act as distributors for merchandise headed south.

Transboundary retail trade is not a one-way street. Although lopsided, this business also benefits the Mexican side, mostly through tourism. This has been especially true for the so-called Gold Coast strip between Tijuana and Ensenada, which has become a prime vacation and retirement destination for Californians. To boost this tourism trade, the Baja California state government is promoting a quality rating system for the hotels and restaurants located on this strip. Increased cross-border trade has also translated into boom times for the red light district in Nuevo Laredo, known alternately as Boys' Town or the Zona de Tolerancia, where some three thousand prostitutes serve mainly U.S. clients.[265]

U.S. residents also go to Mexico border towns for their health. Crossing the border bridges into Mexico, one sees publicity for the ophthalmologists, dentists, and plastic surgeons who have set up offices along the border to serve U.S. consumers. Whether you want a nose job, a new pair of eyeglasses, or a root canal operation, it is cheaper in Mexico. Although the quality of these services might not be as high as in the United States, most clients agree that it is steadily improving. For many the less expensive health and dental services in Mexico offer a way to beat the prohibitive costs of the same care in the United States.

Many also travel to Mexico to get medication restricted or prohibited north of the border. Pharmacists commonly sell over-the-counter drugs and medicine that are available only with a doctor's prescription in the United States. Even when pharmacies do require prescriptions for antibiotics and other drugs, many doctors will gladly write desired prescriptions for a small fee. Although this can benefit border residents who cannot afford a visit to a doctor's office in the United States, self-medication on both side of the border commonly results in drug-related illnesses and medical problems.[266]

Throughout the borderlands the benefits of free trade are obvious. For the region's residents, customs duties and prohibitions make little sense and serve only as annoying obstacles to the free flow of trade and services. Economic integration is not a plan or a prospect; it is a foundation of border life. At the same time, however, there also exists a deep sense of caution about plans to broaden the economic relations between the two countries. In Mexico entrepreneurs worry about the invasion of U.S. retailers and U.S. merchandise. Others agree that more jobs may be coming but they are concerned about the environmental impact of more U.S. investment. In the United States there is also deepening apprehension about the likely environmental repercussions of increased trade and investment, and many fear that open economic borders will facilitate narcotrafficking and quicken the pace of illegal immigration. The most immediate concern on both sides, however, seems to be that the border cities do not have the social and economic infrastructure to handle increased growth.

Everybody's Talking Infrastructure

City officials, *colonia* activists, maquila promoters, and just about everybody else along the border have infrastructure on their minds. Aside from free trade, *infrastructure* is the term probably most commonly used by those discussing public policy and economic development in the border region. Long before presidential candidate Clinton raised the issue of insufficient public-sector investment in infrastructure, borderlanders had recognized that the lack of adequate social and economic infrastructure lay at the heart of their region's development problems.

On both sides of the border, local governments have found themselves unable to respond adequately to the infrastructure shortfalls created by rapid population and industrial growth in the 1970s and 1980s. Throughout the region there is widespread agreement that the border zone is sadly lacking the underlying foundation of social and economic facilities (adequate housing, roads, bridges, wastewater treatment plants, etc.) necessary for continued growth.[267] In public forums, industrial development promoters now echo the calls by environmentalists for better sewage systems, and factory owners nod their heads approvingly when *colonia* residents demand that governments provide improved housing, water facilities, and transportation. Few disagree that a tremendous infrastructure gap faces the region, and most concur that without immediate remedies this critical situation only stands to worsen in the near future, threatening not only the health and welfare of the region's inhabitants but also the ability of corporations to do business profitably.

The infrastructure crisis on the border points to the failure of the kind of economic policies that have guided development on both sides of the border. According to free traders and maquila proponents, economic growth should provide the revenues to cover the infrastructure costs of this development. But on the border this has not occurred. Trade and investment have boomed, but the host communities are suffering from severe infrastructure deficiencies because governments have not used tax and regulatory powers to direct some of the region's profits back into community development.

Further complicating the infrastructure crisis is the confusion about who is responsible for solving the problems. In the United States, border communities that have long promoted maquila-style development and their advantages as gateways to Mexico charge that it is largely a federal issue. For its part the federal government has been willing to assume a certain level of responsibility for border infrastructure, although far below what is needed and what local communities demand. Washington has been still more reluctant to consider the desperate socioeconomic conditions that characterize much of U.S. borderlands as primarily a federal responsibility.

During the 1980s rapid maquila expansion strained the physical infrastructure of border communities. Increased truck traffic, cross-border communications, and daily border crossings underlined the need for more international bridges, customs facilities, and roads.[268] All along the border citizens and businesspeople began griping about backed-up lines at the border, inadequate customs staffing, downtown streets clogged with trucks, and deteriorating connecting roads and bridges. Laredo already prides itself as the country's largest inland port of entry, with fourteen hundred eighteen wheelers rumbling through its city streets each day. On the downside, though, inhabitants of this Texas border town tell stories about being caught in their cars for hours behind long lines of trucks waiting to enter customs. For northbound traffic at major border cities, hour-long delays for traffic to cross through U.S. customs are common.

But that frustration is now often mixed with an excitement about the prospects of free trade. Despite infrastructure nightmares, support for more liberalized trading relations along the border is widespread. Expanded binational trade and investment are predicted to bring more money and jobs for the border communities—a prospect that many along the border find exhilarating.

Free trade also means more competition among the U.S. border cities as they jockey for the lead in the race to attract new cross-border business and trade. San Diego is planning a new binational airport, Brownsville is expanding port facilities and bridges, Laredo is expanding its airport, and McAllen is opening a third international bridge. On the south side of the border, highway upgrades are the priority, including a new toll superhighway connecting the border and the industrial center of Monterrey. Just as the major cities of the border states, such as Monterrey, Chihuahua, and Hermosillo, expect to benefit from expanded binational trade, so, too, do the principal cities of the U.S. Sun Belt. Although they do not sit directly on the border, such cities as San Antonio, Houston, Dallas, Los Angeles, and San Diego are vying to become the distribution, communications, and financial capitals of the new trading bloc. All this means that adequate connecting highways, telecommunications networks, international airports, and border crossings must be in place.

Recognizing their new identities as key players in expanding regional trade, border towns are also demanding that their respective state and federal governments respond to the urgent need for expanded sewage and waste treatment facilities. In the heat of free trade talks, both Washington and Mexico have promised to finance public sanitation infrastructure as part of their mutual commitment to improve border conditions.[269] The concerns expressed by local governments and environmental activists about the public health crisis along the border have spurred the maquila industry and groups like the Border Trade Alliance to join the chorus calling for new wastewater treatment facilities and sewage systems.

Both government and business duly recognize that the crisis concerns the lack of both economic and social infrastructure. Yet the urgent need to upgrade housing, schools, neighborhood water systems, community services, and public health care has generally not received the same level of attention as other infrastructure projects.[270] Carlos Villarreal, Laredo's director of community planning, complained, "There are so many needs here—for housing, development, streets, basic services—and what does Washington build for us? An inspection station. They think of the border only in one way, when they think of it at all."[271]

All agree that more infrastructure is urgently needed along the long-neglected border. But what are the priorities—social or economic projects? And who is going to pay—business or citizens, Mexico or the United States, local or federal governments? Also to consider is the fact that the drive to improve the region's roads, bridges, and public utilities might further whittle away at the fragile resource base of the borderlands. Some large infrastructure projects, especially wastewater treatment plants and sewage systems, will help the border environment and improve border health, but more border crossings, more border bridges, and more and wider roads will impact negatively by increasing the traffic flow through the borderlands. In addressing such matters, the borderlands population will be tackling some of the tougher issues facing both nations in regard to the costs and benefits of closer economic ties.

In all areas of infrastructure, rhetoric and promises have far outstripped real financial commitments. This has been especially true on the U.S. side, where initial promises by the federal government in 1991 to fund $379 million over two years in environmental infrastructure projects turned out to be simply the repackaging of already existing projects.[272] At the same time the Mexican government committed $460 million for environmental and community infrastructure projects over a three-year span. As part of the NAFTA trade negotiations, U.S. and Mexican negotiators proposed the creation of a joint border agency that would issue as much as $8 billion worth of bonds for border cleanup, but it was unclear how much of the onus for repaying the bonds would fall on the private or public sectors.

The International Boundary and Water Commission estimated that wastewater collection and treatment alone will require an investment of nearly $3 billion through 2005. The Border Trade Alliance estimated that nearly $6 billion is needed to pay for all the current infrastructure needs in the U.S. borderlands, while a study by the Northern Border College (COLEF) in Mexico estimated that a $15 billion deficit in needed infrastructure investment had developed in the 1980s.[273] Some environmentalists estimate that border cleanup could cost as much as $30 billion.[274]

Yet another concern is that the infrastructure projects being planned are catch-up projects to satisfy existing needs rather than forward-looking planning that anticipates future growth. Although reluctant to criticize free trade, many community planners and health officials along the border are concerned about the dimensions of the region's expanding infrastructure crisis. Considering that infrastructure financing is already failing to keep pace with present needs, there is concern about just how bad the infrastructure crunch will be if free trade delivers the promised boost in cross-border trade.

Local governments on either side of the border look primarily to the respective federal governments to solve their infrastructure problems. Secondarily they charge the state governments with this responsibility. Both U.S. and Mexican border communities argue that most of their problems are not local but international in origin. Why, they ask, should the burden of facilitating cross-border business fall disproportionately on them?

On the U.S. side, border communities are already experiencing budget woes even before undertaking new infrastructure projects. Being poor, the border towns do not have the tax base to pay for both social and economic infrastructure improvements. The border states, particularly Texas and California, are among the largest exporters to Mexico, but the income generated by these sales flows mostly to bigger, nonborder cities such as Los Angeles, San Antonio, and Houston. Furthermore, the steady flow of Mexicans crossing into their towns severely impacts the local educational, health, and police systems. Given the badly deteriorated condition of local health and education systems, many border residents, including government bureaucrats in charge of social services, are angry that economic infrastructure projects are being given top priority by the local, state, and federal governments.

The financial shortfall is still more pronounced on the Mexican side, where border towns rely almost exclusively on federal revenues. In the past, through programs such as PRONAF, the Mexican government attempted to direct more revenues to the border region to attract tourism, retain a larger portion of transboundary retail trade, and keep the maquila sector content by supplying it with water, electricity, transportation, and other infrastructure needs. Low-cost public utilities, especially electricity, have constituted a de facto government subsidy of industrial development, especially before the public utility price hikes in recent years.

In Mexico the creation of infrastructure is entirely dependent on the federal government since every major tax and spending program—with the exception of property taxes—is channeled through Mexico City. The federal government collects sales, income, and corporate taxes but returns only about 20 percent of the federal budget to the states. The states, in turn, depend on federal revenues for about 80 percent of their annual budgets, with less than one-fourth of these budgets being distributed to the municipalities.[275] The problem here is twofold: the absence of an adequate tax structure in Mexico and the centralism that makes local governments politically and economically dependent on Mexico City. The governor of Baja California Ernesto Ruffo complained, "Look, for every $1.00 in tax revenues that the state sends to Mexico City, we get only 30 cents in return to pay for all public services and infrastructure. It's not fair."[276]

Even if the northern border cities do attempt to plan their communities to ensure that the proper social and economic infrastructure is in place, they have no control over the allocation of funds to finance their projects. As a result, city planning is virtually nonexistent. Tax revenues from border economic activity do flow to Mexico City, but only a small portion of these funds are returned to the border. Yet even if all the revenues were returned, they would still be far less than needed to meet the needs of these booming border towns.

Mexico's public-sector investment has dropped sharply since the 1982 debt crisis, decreasing from about 13 percent of the GDP in 1981 to just 4 percent in 1991. The rapid population and job growth of the borderlands are making the infrastructure gap particularly acute in this region. According to one estimate, infrastructure investment in the northern states is lagging behind job growth by ten years.[277] Despite promises to improve the border infrastructure, Mexico's financial ability to undertake massive new public-sector investment is highly questionable.

The northern border cities are facing the consequences of more than a quarter-century of maquila-based growth. Neither the infrastructure directly used by the maquilas (roads, industrial parks, and public utilities) nor the infrastructure needed by the half-million-member maquila work force (housing, transportation, public utilities, and social services) are paid for by the skimpy tax revenues created by the industry.

For the Mexican government, the in-bond program means forfeiting customs revenue. It also means giving up most tax revenue; because the maquiladoras are set up to earn little or no profit, there is nothing to tax. (Workers' earnings also suffer, since the lack of profit renders meaningless the legal requirement that employers distribute 10 percent of their profits to employees.) Virtually all maquiladoras conduct their in-bond trade among affiliates of the same corporation. The firm has great leeway in setting the prices it likes on the export and import of parts and materials from one affiliate to another, and generally elects to balance them. In this case the in-bond plant's only net revenue on the exchange is the value of the labor employed in Mexico and some overhead expenses. Since this revenue is just enough to cover wages, benefits, and items such as utility costs, the maquiladora shows zero net earnings. The only government income, then, comes from payroll taxes and purchases of electricity, water, waste disposal, and other such services.[278]

To partially redress this problem, the Mexican government imposes a 2 percent Company Asset Tax on foreign-owned and domestic business assets—whether a firm shows net income or not. But the maquiladoras and their lobbyists in Mexico City have succeeded in gaining year-to-year exemptions from this tax since it took effect. The government has also tried to tax foreign citizens working temporarily in Mexico, with an eye on the U.S. engineers and managers who commute or travel occasionally to work in the maquiladora industry. In late 1991 the legislature passed a law taxing nonresident workers on the income they earn from work in Mexico. Again, heavy pressure from the industry forced the government to back off and severely weaken the new tax.[279]

A 1990 study of eighty maquilas in Nuevo Laredo found that together these companies paid only $279,000 in payroll taxes that year—hardly enough to pay for the social services needed by the maquila workers let alone sufficient to cover the costs of infrastructure construction.[280] The maquila industry, however, is quick to complain that the 5 percent payroll tax it pays to subsidize government housing programs has generally not come back to the border.[281] "Tithing to INFONAVIT [the federal housing agency] is like dumping money down a rat hole," complained one maquila manager.[282] Under NAFTA, even the import duties that the maquilas pay will be eliminated.

Business groups like the Border Trade Alliance and the various maquila associations readily acknowledge that weak border infrastructure acts as a constraint on further growth. Infrastructure deficits increase the cost and risk of doing business. Rising public concern about the environmental repercussions of the maquiladoras has pushed the industry to improve its own envi-

ronmental controls while leading to discussions about establishing privately financed infrastructure to supply services and
treat maquila wastes. Responding to social infrastructure problems faced by their workers, some companies sponsor company
housing, child care centers, medical services, and busing. Although generally appreciated by the workers, such initiatives are
undertaken less in the spirit of charity than in the hope that they
will reduce employee absenteeism and improve job performance.

For both ideological and financial reasons, the Mexican government has encouraged the private sector to get into the business of infrastructure projects that would otherwise be the
responsibility of the state. For example, the government has given
concessions to the private sector for the building and management of new toll highways throughout the country. The U.S. government is also inviting the private sector to play a more
prominent role in planning and providing infrastructure.[283]

At a binational conference on the border environment sponsored by the U.S. Environmental Protection Agency and Mexico's
SEDESOL in June 1992, maquila representatives spoke about the
possibility of directly financing new utility districts in Mexico. A
spokesman for General Electric told the conference that his company was pitching in by providing computers, phones, and other
office equipment for SEDESOL. Some industry promoters are also
advancing the idea of having the industrial parks and
maquiladoras establish housing for the workers alongside the assembly plants.[284] InterAmerican Holdings is pushing forward a
plan to create a private binational association that would plan,
develop, and manage a new border crossing and twin city a short
distance from Mexicali/Calexico.

Although appealing to financially strapped local governments,
the concept of having the private sector, particularly the foreign-
owned maquila industry, privatize infrastructure is a dangerous
one on either side of the border. These plans would reinforce the
enclave nature of the maquila industry while raising new questions about the role of government, national sovereignty, and the
dominant role of business. They would also raise questions about
the wisdom of creating "company towns" and the responsibility for
upkeep and repair of facilities should the business benefactors
decide to close up shop or withdraw support for infrastructure
improvements. Privately financed and managed infrastructure, es-

pecially in the face of municipalities with little financial clout, runs the risk of handing de facto planning power over to business. Gabriel Székely, a Mexican scholar at the Center for U.S.-Mexican Studies, has warned that private-sector initiatives may be particularly counterproductive: "In the long term, these are not in the public interest. They are not building this infrastructure in an orderly fashion."[285]

Certainly government needs to bring the private sector into the planning process, and there is no question that business should be paying its fair share for infrastructure improvements. But the private sector cannot be considered the solution to the major infrastructure problems that face the border. Better local and transboundary planning by governments is necessary. Border communities, especially in Mexico, need increased fiscal authority to collect revenues to cover planning and construction costs. On both sides the national governments must recognize that the border infrastructure crisis is as much an international problem as a local one.

In line with the "polluter pays" principle, some members of the U.S. Congress and a number of environmental organizations have suggested that a targeted cross-border tax be imposed on maquila operations to help pay for the cost of border infrastructure or to help Mexico create a better environmental control infrastructure. Others have proposed taxes on all those who profit from free trade to consign a portion of their earnings to cover public health and environmental programs. But free traders have generally criticized such proposals on the ideological grounds that such taxes run counter to the concept of free trade. That may be. But one way or the other, money will have to be found to pay for the social and economic infrastructure needed to ensure that communities teetering on the fulcrum of cross-border business are not its first victims.

References

1. For an extensive history of the border, see Leon C. Metz, *Border: The U.S.-Mexico Line* (El Paso: Mangan Books, 1989). Also see Oscar J. Martínez, *Troublesome Border* (Tucson: University of Arizona Press, 1988). A good brief introduction to the border is Stephen P. Mumme, *United States-Mexico Boundary* (Durham: International Boundaries Research Unit, University of Durham, 1991). Also see the publications of the Institute for Regional Studies of the Californias, San Diego State University.

2. Water consumption in the upper reaches of the Rio Grande has increased so much that the flow of the river from El Paso/Juárez to Presidio/Ojinaga slows to a trickle, and in places the river bed is completely dry.

3. This was the Chamizal dispute, which began in the 1850s and 1860s, when a series of floods and torrential rainfalls caused the channel of the Rio Grande to move south. Assuming that the border had also moved south, the United States assumed jurisdiction of the tract of land. It was not until 1963 that the dispute was finally settled when a concrete channel for the Rio Grande was constructed through El Paso-Juárez and 630 acres were returned to Mexico and another 193 acres came into U.S. possession. Although the settlement was amicable, it came only after a century of binational tensions over the Chamizal tract.

4. J. Moore and H. Pachon, *Hispanics in the United States* (Englewood Cliffs: Prentice-Hall, 1985), as cited in Roberto Ham-Chande and John R. Weeks, "A Demographic Perspective of the U.S.-Mexico Border," in John R. Weeks and Roberto Ham-Chande, eds., *Demographic Dynamics of the U.S.-Mexico Border* (El Paso: Texas Western Press, 1992), 2.

5. There are several human interest books about the borderlands society that describe the cross-border life in all or most of these twin cities, the best of which is Alan Weisman, *La Frontera: The United States Border with Mexico* (San Diego: Harcourt Brace Jovanovich, 1986).

6. Moore and Pachon, *Hispanics in the United States*, 23 (see n. 4).

7. See Jesús Tamayo and José Luis Fernández, *Zonas Fronterizas, México-Estados Unidos* (Mexico City: CIDE, 1983).

8. In Baja California, all of which is a free trade zone, there are no customs checks for ground traffic. These border *municipios* are, from east to west, Matamoros, Río Bravo, Reynosa, G. Díaz Ordaz, Camargo, Miguel Alemán, Miér, Guerrero, Nuevo Laredo, Anáhuac, Hidalgo, Guerrero, Piedras Negras, Jiménez, Ciudad Acuña, Ocampo, Ojinaga, P. G. Guerrero, Guadalupe Bravo, Juárez, Ascensión, Janos, Agua Prieta, Naco, Cananea, Santa Cruz, Nogales, Saríc, Altar, Caborca, Puerto Peñasco, San Luis R.C., Mexicali, Tecate, and Tijuana. Because of the close interaction between these *municipios* with the border economy and society, the Northern Border Development Program in 1985 also included the *municipios* of Ensenada (Baja California), Manuel Benavides (Chihuahua), and Valle Hermoso (Tamaulipas), which do not actually touch the border.

9. Some argue, however, that Nuevo León is not really a border state since it only touches the border for several miles and only 1 percent of its population is found near the border. This compares to 85 percent for Baja California, 42 percent for Tamaulipas, and 31 percent for Chihuahua.

10. From east to west these are Cameron, Hidalgo, Starr, Zapata, Webb, Dimmit, Maverick, Kinney, Val Verde, Terrel, Brewster, Presidio, Jeff Davis, Culberson, Hudspeth, El Paso, Doña Ana, Luna, Hidalgo, Cochise, Santa Cruz, Pima, Yuma, Imperial, and San Diego.

11. Jorge Bustamante, "A Conceptual and Operative Vision of the Population Problems on the Border," in Weeks and Ham-Chande, *Demographic Dynamics*, v (see n. 4).

12. For a valuable discussion of the problems and potential of the IBWC see Stephen P. Mumme, "New Directions in United States-Mexican Transboundary Environmental Management: A Critique of Current Proposals," *Natural Resources Journal* (Summer 1992). Instead of creating new institutions to handle the multitude of environmental and natural resource issues in the borderlands, Mumme argues for a "functional enhancement" approach to current institutional problems. He advocates "taking another look at what is possible within the current management regime with an eye towards extending and institutionalizing that regime in the interest of both nations and the border environment."

13. Commission for the Study of International Migration and Cooperative Economic Development, *Unauthorized Migration: An Economic Development Response* (Washington, DC, 1990), 104.

14. Rene M. Zenteno Quintero and Rodolfo Cruz Piñero, "A Geodemographic Definition of the Mexican Northern Border," in Weeks and Ham-Chande, *Demographic Dynamics*, 19 (see n. 4).

15. Ideas of a changing cultural landscape along the border are drawn from a talk delivered by Lawrence Herzog at the University of New Mexico's Latin American Institute, 1 Oct. 1992.

16. Lawrence A. Herzog, "Transboundary Ecosystem Management in the San Diego-Tijuana Region," in Oscar J. Martínez, ed., *Across Boundaries: Transborder Interaction in Comparative Perspective* (El Paso: Texas Western Press, 1986), 97-115.

17. Lawrence A. Herzog, *Where North Meets South: Cities, Space, and Politics on the United States-Mexico Border* (Austin: University of Texas Press, 1990).

18. These are Tijuana, Baja California/San Ysidro-San Diego, California; Mexicali, Baja California/Calexico, California; San Luis Rio Colorado, Sonora/Yuma, Arizona; Nogales, Sonora/Nogales, Arizona; Agua Prieta, Sonora/Douglas, Arizona; Naco, Sonora/Naco, Arizona; Las Palomas, Chihuahua/Columbus, New Mexico; Ciudad Juárez, Chihuahua/El Paso, Texas; Ojinaga, Chihuahua/Presidio, Texas; Ciudad Acuña, Coahuila/Del Rio, Texas; Piedras Negras, Coahuila/Eagle Pass, Texas; Nuevo Laredo, Tamaulipas/Laredo, Texas; Reynosa, Tamaulipas/McAllen, Texas; and Matamoros, Tamaulipas/Brownsville, Texas. Six main twin cities account for 96 percent of the urban population on the U.S. side and 84 percent on the Mexican side. These are Brownsville/Matamoros, McAllen/Reynosa, Laredo/Nuevo Laredo, El Paso/Ciudad Juárez, Mexicali/Calexico, and San Diego/Tijuana.

19. Weeks and Ham-Chande, *Demographic Dynamics*, 6 (see n. 4).

20. Official population statistics are particularly unreliable for Mexican border cities, where the population in sprawling *colonias* is consistently underestimated.

21. Weeks and Ham-Chande, *Demographic Dynamics*, 19 (see n. 4).

22. This concept of the changing function of the border is drawn from the work of Lawrence A. Herzog, especially Lawrence A. Herzog, ed., *Changing Boundaries in the Americas: New Perspectives on the U.S.-Mexican, Central American, and South American Borders* (San Diego: Center for U.S.-Mexican Studies, 1992), 3-12.

23. In 1990 the poverty line was defined as a "minimum needs threshold" of $13,359 per year for a family of four.

24. Figures from the Center for Entrepreneurial Development, University of Texas at El Paso.

25. Hispanic Policy Development Project, Inc., *A More Perfect Union: Achieving Hispanic Parity by the Year 2000, A Report from the 1989 and 1990 Aspen Institute Conferences* (Aspen, CO: Aspen Institute, 1991).

26. Mercedes Pedrero Nieto, "The Economically Active Population in the Northern Region of Mexico," in Weeks and Ham-Chande, *Demographic Dynamics*, 214 (see n. 4).

27. James Pick and Edgar Butler, "Socioeconomic Inequality in the U.S./Mexico Borderlands: Modernization and Buffering," *Frontera Norte* 2, no. 3 (Jan.-June 1990).

28. Linda S. Peterson and Eduardo E. Arriaga, "Comparative Sociodemographic Indicators at the U.S.-Mexico Border," in Weeks and Ham-Chande, *Demographic Dynamics*, 69 (see n. 4).

29. Leopoldo Núñez Fernández, "Estimates of Infant Mortality for the Northern Border of Mexico," in Weeks and Ham-Chande, *Demographic Dynamics*, 152 (see n. 4).

30. Minimum wage is set by the federal government to match the cost of living in different regions. The minimum wage along the border is the same as in Mexico City.

31. "Cheap Labor Festers in Mexico's Hong Kong," *Arizona Republic*, 16 April 1989.

32. *Rural Development: Problems and Progress of Colonia Subdivisions Near the Mexican Border* (Washington, DC: General Accounting Office, Nov. 1990).

33. Jane Grandolfo, "Border Crisis: Prosperity Plan a Bust in Poverty-Ridden Juárez," *Houston Post*, 2 July 1989.

34. For a good description of northern Mexico's history, see Martínez, *Troublesome Border*, 106-23 (see n. 1).

35. Interview with Victor Clark Alfaro, 24 April 1991. For more information on this "economy of discards" in the northern borderlands, see Joan Anderson and Martin de la Rosa, "Economic Strategies of Poor Families on the Mexican Border," *Journal of Borderlands Studies* 6, no. 1 (Spring 1991).

36. Carlos Monsiváis, "Los Angeles: Heart of the Mexican Dream," *New Perspectives Quarterly* (Winter 1991).

37. The number of Latinos is probably underestimated given the low counts of undocumented residents and those Latinos living in major urban areas.

38. Statistical information from Jeffrey S. Passel, "Demographic Profile," *Report on the Americas* 26, no. 2 (Sept. 1992).

39. Figures from U.S. Bureau of the Census, as cited in Marta Lopez-Garza, "Los Angeles: Ascendant Chicano Power," *Report on the Americas*, Sept. 1992, 34.

40. Cited in David Rieff, *Los Angeles: Capital of the Third World* (New York: Simon and Schuster, 1991), 155.

41. For a provocative discussion of the impact of the Voting Rights Act on Latino politics, see: Peter Skerry, *Mexican Americans: The Ambivalent Minority* (New York: The Free Press, 1993).

42. Raúl Hinojosa-Ojeda, Sherman Robinson, and Goetz Wolff, *The Impact of a North American Free Trade Agreement on California: A Summary of Key Research Findings* (Los Angeles: UCLA Lewis Center for Regional Policy Studies, Sept. 1992), 5.

43. Work force figures from Saskia Sassen, "Why Migration?" *Report on the Americas* 26, no. 1 (July 1992):19.

44. What academics over the past few decades have called the "Battle of the Name" was revived in 1992 by the results of the Latino National Political Survey, which concluded that the term American was preferred over Latino or Hispanic by most of the Mexican, Cuban, and Puerto Rican-descent respondents. According to the directors of the sur-

vey, "To the extent that the Hispanic political community exists, there is scant evidence that it is rooted in alleged distinctive cultural traditions such as Spanish-language maintenance, religiosity, or shared identity. Mexicans, Puerto Ricans, and Cubans have little interaction with each other, most do not recognize that they have much in common culturally, and they do not profess strong affection for each other." The publication of the survey stirred wide debate among Latino leaders, some of whom believed that the survey questions were presented in such a way to confirm the conservative views of the survey sponsors. But for many others the survey confirmed that attempts to build a Latino political consensus may be based on faulty assumptions. See Rodolfo O. de la Garza et al., eds., *Latino Voices: Mexican, Puerto Rican, and Cuban Perspectives on American Politics* (Boulder, CO: Westview Press, 1992), 13, 14.

45. For a provocative discussion of standardized terminology, see Martha E. Gimenez, "Latino/Hispanic—Who Needs a Name? The Case against a Standardized Terminology," *International Journal of Health Services* 19, no. 3 (1989). She argues that the Hispanic label imputes to Latin Americans a contrived Hispanic ethnicity while classifying as minorities people who historically have never been oppressed as such in the United States. Instead she advocates the broader use of theoretical and descriptive categories of analysis related to social class, minority groups, national origin, and socioeconomic status.

46. U.S. Department of Commerce, Census Bureau, Ethnic and Hispanic Branch, 1990 Census Special Tabulations. The corresponding figures for the two other border states were 57 percent in New Mexico and 17 percent in Arizona. In New Mexico, the relatively low Mexico-origin figure is accounted for by the high percentage in the category of "other-Hispanic origin."

47. According to U.S. Decennial Census 1990, the top states by Latino percentage of state population and percentage of U.S. Latinos (respectively) are: California, 25.8, 24.4; Texas, 25.5, 19.4; New York, 12.3, 9.9; Florida, 12.2, 7.0; Illinois, 7.9, 4.0; New Jersey, 9.6, 3.3; Arizona, 18.8, 3.1; New Mexico, 38.2, 2.6; Colorado, 12.9, 1.9.

48. David Hayes-Bautista, Werner Schink, and Jorge Chapa, "The Young Latino Population in an Aging American Society," in Jorge Bustamante, Clark Reynolds, and Raúl Hinojosa, eds., *U.S.-Mexican Relations: Labor Market Interdependence* (Stanford: Stanford University Press, 1992), 27.

49. Martinez, *Troublesome Border*, 95 (see n. 1).

50. Ibid., 95-96.

51. One explanation of the term *Chicano* is that it comes from *mechicano*, the Nahuatl (or Aztec) pronunciation of the Spanish word describing people living in Mexico. F. Chris Garcia and Rudolph O. de la Garza, *The Chicano Political Experience: Three Perspectives* (North Scituate, MA: Duxbury Press, 1977), 14-16.

52. Martinez, *Troublesome Border*, 96 (see n. 1).

53. Aztlán was the legendary place of origin of the Aztecs, the site of seven caves where the Aztec empire was born.

54. Vasconcelos, who served as the rector of the national university and as one of revolutionary Mexico's first education ministers, popularized this concept in his book *La tesis de la raza cósmica*. He wrote that "we will succeed in the Americas [not including in his concept the United States or Canada], before anywhere else in the globe has come near, in creating a new race, fashioned out of the treasures of all the other races: The final race, the cosmic race."

55. The respective figures for Latinos of different national origins are: 20 percent for Mexican origin; 30 percent for Puerto Rican origin; 12 percent for Cuban origin; 17 percent for Central and South American origin; and 16 percent for other origins. *The Hispanic Population of the United States* (Washington, DC: U.S. Bureau of the Census, March 1990) and *Current Population Reports*, no. 449 (March 1991), table 4.

56. Hispanic Policy Development Project, Inc., *A More Perfect Union* (see n. 25).

57. Hinojosa-Ojeda et al., *The Impact of a North American Free Trade Agreement* (see n. 42). Also affected by international immigration, global restructuring, and free trade are U.S. blacks, who have seen manufacturing jobs leave their cities and the low-wage job market cornered by immigrants. An alarmist but nonetheless important view of immigration's impact on Los Angeles blacks is Jack Miles, "Blacks vs. Browns," *Atlantic Monthly*, Oct. 1992. "The almost total absence of black gardeners, busboys, chambermaids, nannies, janitors, and construction workers in a city with a notoriously large pool of unemployed, unskilled black people leaps to the eye," wrote Miles.

58. Quoted in Diana Solis, "Trade Pact Puts Mexican Americans in a Dilemma over Jobs in Border Area," *Wall Street Journal*, 7 Aug. 1992.

59. *Voting and Registration in the Election of November 1992* (Washington, DC: U.S. Bureau of the Census, 1993).

60. More than 90 percent of Latino elected officials are Democrats, but the Republican Party since the 1980 election has made strong inroads into the Latino community. Forty-four percent of Latino voters supported Ronald Reagan in 1984 and 35 percent supported George Bush in 1988.

61. Annette Fuente, "New York: Elusive Unity in La Gran Manzana," *Report on the Americas* 26, no. 2 (Sept. 1992):27-33.

62. On the differences within the Latino community see Earl Shorris, "Latinos: The Complexity of Identity," *Report on the Americas* 26, no. 2 (Sept. 1992):19-26.

63. De la Garza et al., *Latino Voices*, 14 (see n. 44). The authors suggest that a common Hispanic political agenda could perhaps be developed around a liberal domestic agenda since most survey respondents did indicate their support for increased government involvement in solving social problems.

64. Many of these arguments were presented in Gov. Richard D. Lamm and Gary Imoff, *The Immigration Time Bomb: The Fragmenting of America* (New York: E.P. Dutton, 1985). The main national immigration-reform organization is the Federation for American Immigration Reform (FAIR).

65. See George J. Borjas, *Friends or Strangers: The Impact of Immigrants on the U.S. Economy* (New York: Basic Books, 1990), and Julian L. Simon, *The Economic Consequences of Immigration* (Cambridge, MA: Basil Blackwell, 1989).

66. See Jeffrey S. Passel, "Undocumented Migration," *Annals of the American Academy of Political Social Science*, no. 487 (Sept. 1986):181-200, and Gregory de Freitas, "The Effects of Recent Immigrants on American Workers," *Migration World* 16, no. 1 (1986):7-15.

67. Whether undocumented immigrants use more in public services than they contribute in taxes is an extremely difficult question to answer. Local, state, and federal services and tax revenues are variously affected, and data collection is hampered by the informal nature of many jobs held by undocumented workers. One estimate that argues that the overall economic benefit of undocumented workers "probably outweigh[s] the economic costs of fiscal deficits" is given by Thomas J. Espenshade and Tracy Ann Goodis in testimony before the Subcommittee on Economic Resources, Competitiveness, and Security Economics of the Joint Economic Committee, *Economic Consequences of Immigration*, 22 May 1986. For a case study of the perception of crime caused by undocumented immigrants, see Daniel Wolf, *Undocumented Aliens and Crime: The Case of San Diego County* (San Diego: Center for U.S.-Mexican Studies, 1988).

68. Augie Bareño, "A Local Perspective on Free Trade," in Paul Ganster and Eugenio O. Valenciano, eds., *The Mexican-U.S. Border Region and the Free Trade Agreement* (San Diego: Institute for Regional Studies of the Californias, San Diego State University, 1992), 9.

69. One of the best overviews of the place of Mexican immigrant workers in U.S. society and economy is James Cockcroft, *Outlaws in the Promised Land: Mexican Immigrant Workers and America's Future* (New York: Grove Press, 1986).

70. Deportation campaigns occurred in the early 1920s, the early 1930s, the mid-1950s, and the mid-1970s. The most important immigration reforms have been:

    – The 1924 Immigration Act, establishing an immigration quota system based on nationality but exempting western hemisphere countries, including Mexico. It also required all immigrants to have valid visas, placing the first legal restriction on casual migration from Mexico to the United States. The act also established the U.S. Border Patrol.

    – The 1942 *bracero* program, providing U.S. employers with legally contracted Mexican workers.

    – The cancellation of the *bracero* program in 1964.

    – The Immigration and Nationality Act amendments of 1965, which established a quota for immigration from western hemisphere countries. Immediate relatives of U.S. citizens—spouses, unmarried children under twenty-one years of age, and parents of adult citizens—and certain skilled workers were exempted from the quotas. The amendments also required the U.S. secretary of labor to find that a prospective immigrant would not adversely affect the jobs of U.S. workers before a visa could be issued.

    – The 1976 establishment of a quota of 20,000 visas for Mexican immigrants. The exemptions established in 1965 continued to apply.

    – The 1986 Immigration Reform and Control Act (IRCA) establishing sanctions for employers of undocumented foreigners and providing legal status for foreigners residing in the United States continuously since Jan. 1982. It also provided legal status to agricultural workers who had worked a minimum number of days in the previous three years.

    – The Immigration Act of 1990, which expanded the quota for total legal immigration from 270,000 per year to 340,000 per year. "Independent" visas—those granted for job-related or investment reasons—were separated from "family preference" visas so that applicants in the two categories would not compete with each other. Nearly all the quota increase was allocated to independent visas, but within the family-preference category, the quota for immediate relatives of permanent residents was doubled. This change was a direct response to the increased numbers of legal permanent residents resulting from IRCA's legalization provisions. Immediate relatives of U.S. citizens continued to be exempted from any quota.

71. The classic account of the Mexican experience in the United States during this period is Carey McWilliams, *North from Mexico* (New York: Greenwood Press, 1968).

72. This point is explored in detail in Cockcroft, *Outlaws in the Promised Land* (see n. 69).

73. From 1948 to 1951 no formal agreement was in effect, but the program continued on an informal basis with employers directly recruiting workers. In 1951 Congress enacted PL-78, which eliminated the Mexican government's role and downgraded that of the U.S. government from labor contractor to program regulator.

74. *Statistical Yearbook of the Immigration and Naturalization Service, 1990* (Washington, DC: U.S. Immigration and Naturalization Service, 1991).

75. The changing composition of Mexican immigrant workers is described in Wayne A. Cornelius, "Los migrantes de la crisis: El nuevo perfil de la migración de mano de obra mexicana a California en los años ochenta," in Gail Mummert, ed., *Población y trabajo en contextos regionales* (Zamora, Michoacán: El Colegio de Michoacán, 1990).

76. Fernando Lozano Ascencio, *Bringing It Back Home: Remittances to Mexico from Migrant Workers in the United States* (San Diego: Center for U.S.-Mexican Studies, 1993).

77. A great number of studies on this topic have been carried out. The conclusions of nineteen such studies are summarized in Jorge Durand and Douglas S. Massey, "Mexican Migration to the United States," *Latin American Research Review* 27, no. 2

(1992). Durand and Massey note that a minority of studies have found significant productive investment resulting from remittances. The contradictory findings probably reflect the varying conditions of the towns and cities to which the remittances are sent.

78. This concept is developed in Eric Wolf, *Europe and the People without History* (Berkeley: University of California Press, 1982).

79. Sassen, "Why Migration?" 14 (see n. 43). Also see two excellent studies by Sassen of the impact of global restructuring: *The Mobility of Labor and Capital: A Study in International Investment and Labor Flow* (Cambridge: Cambridge University Press, 1988) and *The Global City* (Princeton: Princeton University Press, 1992).

80. Sassen, "Why Migration?" 15 (see n. 43).

81. For analysis about capital-labor collaboration, see Beth Sims, *Workers of the World Undermined: American Labor's Role in U.S. Foreign Policy* (Boston: South End Press, 1992), and Daniel Cantor and Juliet Schor, *Tunnel Vision: Labor, the World Economy, and Central America* (Boston: South End Press, 1987).

82. See, for example, Wayne Cornelius, "One Way Travel to the U.S. on the Rise," *Hemisfile* 2, no. 2 (March 1991).

83. Richard Mines, Beatriz Boccalandro, and Susan Gabbard, "The Latinization of U.S. Farm Labor," *Report on the Americas* 26, no. 1 (July 1992):43. Two out of five U.S. farm workers are migrants, meaning they travel seventy-five miles or more for their work.

84. Peter Francese, "Aging America Needs Foreign Blood," *Wall Street Journal*, 27 March 1990.

85. Douglas S. Massey, "The Settlement Process among Mexican Migrants to the U.S.," *American Sociology Review* 51 (Oct. 1986):670-84.

86. David Ronfeldt, "Free Trade and Immigration Issues," in Ganster and Valenciano, *The Mexican-U.S. Border Region*, 66 (see n. 68).

87. Georges Vernez and David Ronfeldt, "The Current Situation in Mexican Immigration," *Science*, 8 March 1991, 1189. Also see Durand and Massey, "Mexican Migration" (n. 77).

88. In 1975 INS chief Leonard Chapman warned that the United States faced a "vast and silent invasion of illegal aliens."

89. Quoted in *Newsweek*, 25 Jan. 1984.

90. The Centro Binacional de Derechos Humanos in Tijuana has documented the widespread extortion and human rights abuses of migrants. See Victor Clark Alfaro, *Los aspirantes a indocumentados: Una fuente segura de ingresos, el caso de Tijuana* (Tijuana: Centro Binacional de Derechos Humanos, 1988).

91. Survey conducted by Colegio de la Frontera Norte in Nogales, cited in Francisco Lara Valencia, "Programa Paisano: Problemas y retos en Sonora," *La voz del norte* 11 (June 1990).

92. Understandably, the Mexican government is reluctant to cooperate with the INS in halting the flow of its own citizenry. But Mexican immigration authorities have been encouraged and assisted by the INS in a campaign to obstruct the stream of migrants from Central America. Mexico's interior ministry joined the INS, DEA, and the CIA in Operation Hold the Line, which among other things employed undercover agents to infiltrate the clandestine network that helps migrants enter the United States. In large part because of this cooperative relationship with the INS along Mexico's southern border, which includes INS training and intelligence sharing, the number of Central Americans that Mexico stops on the Guatemala border has steadily increased. In 1990 Mexico deported more than 110,000 Central Americans. See Bill Frelick, *Update on Interdiction of Central Americans in Mexico* (Washington, DC: U.S. Committee on Refugees, 16 July 1991); *Running the Gauntlet: The Central American Journey to Mexico*

(Washington, DC: U.S. Committee for Refugees, Jan. 1991); Leo Chavez, Estevan Flores, and Maria López-Graza, "Migrants and Settlers: Comparison of Undocumented Mexicans and Central Americans in the United States," *Frontera Norte* 1, no. 1 (Tijuana, Jan.-June 1989). Chavez et al. make the point that most Central Americans leave their countries with the intention of returning someday, whereas Mexicans increasingly are interested in settling permanently in the United States.

93. *Sealing Our Borders: The Human Toll* (Philadelphia: American Friends Service Committee, Feb. 1992), 6.

94. Interview with Rubén García, director of Annunciation House, 29 Nov. 1991.

95. Americas Watch, *Brutality Unchecked: Human Rights Abuses along the U.S. Border with Mexico* (New York, May 1992).

96. *Sealing Our Borders*, 10 (see n. 93).

97. Figures compiled by the U.S.-Mexico Border Program of the AFSC in San Diego.

98. *Immigration Control: Immigration Policies Affect INS Detention Efforts* (Washington, DC: General Accounting Office, June 1992). Criminal aliens are defined as those charged with breaking other than immigration laws. The two other main INS categories are deportable aliens and excludable aliens.

99. San Diego Association of Governments, *The Impact of Undocumented Aliens on the Criminal Justice System* (San Diego, Oct. 1986), 5.

100. Wolf, *Undocumented Aliens and Crime*, 23 (see n. 67).

101. Ibid., vii.

102. Wayne Kirkpatrick, U.S. Border Patrol, quoted in ibid., 40.

103. IRCA granted "amnesty" to 1.8 million undocumented residents, of whom 1.2 million were Mexican citizens. The act also legalized the status of 1.3 million migrants claiming to be temporary agricultural workers. Of these, one million were Mexican.

104. Prior to IRCA, immigration law referred only to illegal entry and presence, not to employment. Undocumented workers enjoyed the same rights as nonimmigrant workers. For detailed discussions of undocumented immigrants' post-IRCA legal rights, see Linda S. Bosniak, "Exclusion and Membership: The Dual Identity of the Undocumented Worker under United States Law," *Wisconsin Law Review* (1988):955-1042, and Robin Alexander, "Labor Rights Protections after IRCA," *Immigration Newsletter* 17, no. 1. Examples of IRCA's effect on labor rights are given in María Blanco and Pauline Kim, *How Employer Sanctions Undermine the Enforcement of Federal Labor Laws* (San Francisco: Equal Rights Advocates, n.d.). All three of these resources are cited in Cathi Tactaquin, "What Rights for the Undocumented?" *Report on the Americas* 26, no. 1 (July 1992).

105. Peter A. Schey, "North American Economic Integration: A Multilateral Approach to Migration and the Human Rights of Migrant Workers," paper presented at the 16th Annual Conference on Immigration and Naturalization at the University of Texas at Austin School of Law, San Antonio, Texas, 17-18 Sept. 1992.

106. For a classic example of this reasoning, see The Council of Economic Advisers, *Economic Report of the President, Transmitted to Congress, February 1986* (Washington, DC: Government Printing Office, 1986), especially Chapter Seven, "The Economic Effects on Immigration." See also *The Effects of Immigration of the U.S. Economy and Labor Market* (Washington, DC: U.S. Department of Labor, Bureau of International Labor Affairs, 1989). For a survey of the role of Mexican labor in nine varied sectors of the U.S. economy, see Wayne A. Cornelius, ed., *The Changing Role of Mexican Labor in the U.S. Economy* (San Diego: Center for U.S.-Mexican Studies, forthcoming). A review of twenty-five methodologically varied studies of the labor market impact of undocumented workers is given in Frank D. Bean, Edward E. Telles, and B. Lindsay Lowell, "Undocumented Migration to the United States: Perceptions and Evidence," *Population and Development Review* 13 (Dec. 1987).

107. See James E. Pearce and Jeffrey W. Gunther, "Illegal Immigration from Mexico: Effects on the Texas Economy," *Southwest Journal of Business and Economics* 6 (Winter-Spring 1989), and David Hensley, "The Impacts of Immigration Reform on the California Economy," *Labor Law Journal* (Aug. 1989).

108. Personal communication from Philip Martin, a farm labor economist at the University of California, Davis.

109. For an insightful article on the social effects of this tension, see Miles, "Blacks vs. Browns," 41-68 (n. 57).

110. *Immigration Reform: Employer Sanctions and the Question of Discrimination* (Washington, DC: General Accounting Office, 1990). The GAO found that employer discrimination based on national origin constitutes "a serious pattern of discrimination." Ten percent of employers surveyed by the GAO reported that they began to discriminate on the basis of a person's foreign appearance or accent, and 9 percent indicated they began to discriminate on the basis of a person's citizenship status. These numbers are low-end estimates, since many employers may not have wanted to disclose that they discriminated in their hiring practices.

111. See Philip Martin, *Harvest of Confusion: Migrant Workers in U.S. Agriculture* (Boulder, CO: Westview Press, 1988), 131-35.

112. The Census Bureau does not collect information about the legal status of U.S. inhabitants. The most common method of estimating undocumented immigrants is to subtract the INS' number of legal foreign-born residents from the Census Bureau's number of total foreign-born residents, after attempting to correct for misreporting during the Census. Robert Warren and Jeffrey S. Passel describe this procedure and their results using 1980 Census figures in "A Count of the Uncountable: Estimates of Undocumented Aliens Counted in the 1980 United States Census," *Demography* 24, no. 3 (Aug. 1987). Data from the 1980 Mexican census—in which respondents who reside or have resided in the United States have no reason to lie about their legal status—led Passel (in 1985) to estimate that 1.9 million undocumented Mexicans resided in the United States.

113. Quoted in Benjamin Shore, "Low-key Attitude Shift Favors Getting Tough on Immigration," *San Diego Union-Tribune*, 26 Sept. 1992.

114. An econometric study by University of California researchers indicates that 610,000 people are likely to migrate from Mexico to the United States if Mexican corn subsidies are removed and U.S.-Mexican agricultural trade is opened. See Sherman Robinson et al., *Agricultural Policies and Migration in a U.S.-Mexico Free Trade Area: A Computable General Equilibrium Analysis*, working paper no. 617 (Berkeley: U.S. Department of Agriculture and Resource Economics, 1991). Luis Téllez, Mexico's undersecretary of agriculture, estimated that as many as fourteen million people will migrate from rural areas to urban areas between 1990 and 2010. Tim Golden, "The Dream of Land Dies Hard in Mexico," *New York Times*, 27 Nov. 1991, A1.

115. Wayne A. Cornelius and Philip L. Martin, *The Uncertain Connection: Free Trade and Mexico-U.S. Migration* (San Diego: Center for U.S.-Mexican Studies, 1993), 33, citing Mexican government estimates.

116. See David Clark Scott, "Free Trade and Mexican Migrants," *Christian Science Monitor*, 15 June 1992.

117. Sassen, *The Mobility of Labor and Capital* (see n. 79).

118. For a good summary of the main arguments that hold that a free trade agreement will not increase immigration over the short and medium term, see Cornelius and Martin, *The Uncertain Connection* (see n. 115). The authors acknowledge that disruptions in Mexico's agricultural economy will likely result in increased immigration in the short term but argue that "trade-linked development" has the best chance of slowing emigration rates from Mexico in the long run. They assert that additional emigration from

rural Mexico owing to NAFTA-related economic restructuring has been overestimated, noting that many rural dwellers have already diversified their income sources, that increased internal migration rates do not necessarily mean increased emigration, and that new U.S. agricultural investment in Mexico may create additional jobs just as U.S. fruit and vegetable production in the United States increased in the 1980s.

119. Cited in William Branigan, "Violence, Tensions Increasing along the U.S.-Mexican Border," *New York Times*, 25 June 1990.

120. Proposals for an international agreement protecting the rights of immigrant workers have been put forth. See, for example, Schey, "North American Economic Integration" (n. 105).

121. Weisman, *La Frontera*, 25 (see n. 5). In the mid-1980s Starr County received national attention and notoriety as the extent of local involvement in the drug trade came to light. From top to bottom, the county's elected officials and government agencies participated in the drug trade in one way or another. Before the system was broken up through law enforcement efforts, even the county road crews received payoffs for blading airstrips needed by drug smugglers. Interview with Mike Gallagher, *Albuquerque Journal*, 4 Sept. 1992.

122. Most of the discussion of early contraband traffic on the border is drawn from Terrence E. Poppa, *Drug Lord: The Life and Death of a Mexican Kingpin* (New York: Pharos Books, 1990).

123. For a discussion of these trading relationships, see Weisman, *La Frontera* (n. 5). Weisman's interviews along the U.S.-Mexican border during the mid-1980s showed that even Mexican government agencies took advantage of the quicker pace of import transactions that were concluded outside authorized Mexican Customs channels.

124. See Douglas Clark Kinder, "Nativism, Cultural Conflict, Drug Control: United States and Latin American Antinarcotics Diplomacy through 1965," in Donald J. Mabry, ed., *The Latin American Narcotics Trade and U.S. National Security* (New York: Greenwood Press, 1989), 13.

125. William O. Walker III, *Drug Control in the Americas* (Albuquerque: University of New Mexico Press, 1981), 58.

126. Report of the Bilateral Commission on the Future of United States-Mexican Relations, *The Challenge of Interdependence: Mexico and the United States* (Lanham, MD: University Press of America, 1989), 123. For a less sanguine view of white America's perceptions of the Hispanic community and marijuana consumption, see Kinder, "Nativism, Cultural Conflict, Drug Control," 15-16 (see n. 124).

127. On Mexico's concerns about traffic in and domestic use of opiates during the early twentieth century, see Walker, *Drug Control in the Americas*, 22, 37, 58 (n. 125).

128. Report of the Bilateral Commission, *The Challenge of Interdependence*, 125 (see n. 126).

129. Ibid., 12.

130. The figures are from the U.S.-government-sponsored National Narcotics Intelligence Consumers Committee. Cited in ibid., 124-26.

131. Although Mexico contributes nearly two-thirds of the marijuana imported to the U.S. market, it is not the major source of pot smoked in the United States. That achievement is claimed by domestic producers in the United States, where marijuana is grown nearly nationwide. The National Narcotics Intelligence Consumers Committee (NNICC, pronounced "nick") is an interagency effort of the U.S. government. Members include federal agencies responsible for policy development, intelligence gathering, research, and law enforcement. The annual NNICC Report estimates global drug production and reports eradication and interdiction figures. The figures are from National Narcotics Intelligence Consumers Committee, *The NNICC Report 1991: The Supply of*

Illicit Drugs to the United States (Washington, DC: Drug Enforcement Administration, July 1992), 46.

132. The percentage given is based on qualitative analysis of 600 samples of heroin seized during interdiction operations in 1991. According to Bob Rae, coordinator of the NNICC, this figure—as well as all estimates of illegal drug availability—must be taken only as a general indicator of a given drug's availability and source. Regional variations will reflect different totals, depending on which countries tend to supply given areas, and the limited sample size—in which large and small samples are rated equally—may distort real national totals. Interview with Bob Rae, Office of Intelligence, Drug Enforcement Administration, 9 Sept. 1992. For more information on the methodology used by the NNICC to estimate Mexican heroin's share of the U.S. market, see ibid., 23-24.

133. *International Narcotics Control Strategy Report* (Washington, DC: U.S. Department of State, Bureau of International Narcotics Matters, June 1991).

134. *Department of State Bulletin*, Oct. 1989.

135. President's Commission on Organized Crime, Report to the President and the Attorney General, *America's Habit: Drug Abuse, Drug Trafficking, and Organized Crime* (Washington, DC: Government Printing Office, 1986).

136. Samuel I. del Villar, "The Illicit U.S.-Mexico Drug Market: Failure of Policy and an Alternative," in Riordan Roett, ed., *Mexico and the United States: Managing the Relationship* (Boulder, CO: Westview Press, 1988), 192.

137. "Drugs in Mexico," *Latin America Weekly Report*, 12 Dec. 1991.

138. Peter Reuter, *Eternal Hope: America's International Narcotics Effort* (Santa Monica, CA: Rand Corporation, 1987), cited in Samuel I. del Villar, "Rethinking Hemispheric Antinarcotics Strategy and Security," in Mabry, *The Latin American Narcotics Trade*, 106 (see n. 124).

139. Quoted in *Drug Control: U.S.-Mexico Opium Poppy and Marijuana Aerial Eradication Program* (Washington, DC: General Accounting Office, Jan. 1988), 19-20. *Campesinos* who worked as field labor for *El Búfalo*, a marijuana-growing, storage, and processing complex in Chihuahua, earned about $6 for a day's work in 1984. The complex, which handled marijuana grown throughout Mexico for Guadalajara kingpin Rafael Caro Quintero and a syndicate of his associates, utilized state-of-the art agribusiness techniques. Elaine Shannon, *Desperados: Latin Drug Lords, U.S. Lawmen, and the War America Can't Win* (New York: Viking, 1988), 195.

140. The figures cited are from the mid-1970s. Peter A. Lupsha, "Drug Trafficking: Mexico and Colombia in Comparative Perspective," *Journal of International Affairs* (1981):97.

141. National Narcotics Intelligence Consumers Committee, *The NNICC Report 1991*, 46 (see n. 131).

142. *International Narcotics Control Strategy Report* (Washington, DC: U.S. Department of State, Bureau of International Narcotics Matters, March 1991), 162.

143. Weisman, *La Frontera*, 28 (see n. 5).

144. Quoted in Shannon, *Desperados*, 346 (see n. 139). This sort of patronage has bought loyalty and admiration from some in Mexico. In the highlands of Sinaloa, there is even a shrine to Jesús Malverde, a bandit hanged in 1909. Revered as something of a Robin Hood, Malverde is now considered the patron saint of traffickers and exploited peasants alike. Larry Rohter, "In a Most Unsaintly City, a Bandit Wears a Halo," *New York Times*, 11 May 1989.

145. Interview with Dick Kamp, Border Ecology Project, 4 Feb. 1991.

146. Steven Strasser, "The Southwest Drug Connection," *Newsweek*, 23 Nov. 1987.

147. Cited in Mark T. Sullivan, "Drug Money Fills Vacuum in Strapped Border Towns," *San Diego Union-Tribune*, 30 Nov. 1990. The effect of drug money can be seen in the inte-

riors of Mexico and the United States as well. José Leonardo Contreras Subias, a top Mexican trafficker wanted in connection with the murder of U.S. drug enforcement agent Enrique Camarena, moved into Atoka, Oklahoma, in the mid-1980s. He bought land at generous prices to help ranchers who were facing bankruptcy after the crash in land prices. He hired ranch hands and paid them well, purchased vehicles and farm equipment, and otherwise used his money to buy loyalty—or at least blindness to his activities. When he was finally arrested, police discovered that he had been laundering money by buying real estate in Texas, Oklahoma, and Salt Lake City. Kevin Kelly, "The Oklahoma Town that Drug Money Bought," *Business Week*, 23 May 1988.

148. Interview with Gallagher (see n. 121).

149. Report of the Bilateral Commission, *The Challenge of Interdependence*, 126 (see n. 126).

150. Statement of Thomas A. McDermott, senior agent in charge, U.S. Customs Service, Arizona, in a hearing before the U.S. Senate Committee on Appropriations, *The Frontline of the U.S. War on Drugs: The Southwest Border*, 101st Cong., 1st sess., 1990, 32.

151. Craig Pyes, "The War of the Flowers," *Oui*, 10 Oct. 1977.

152. Shannon, *Desperados*, 343 (see n. 139).

153. McDermott before hearing, *The Frontline of the U.S. War on Drugs* (see n. 150).

154. Poppa's *Drug Lord* (n. 122) describes the day-to-day reality of life in Ojinaga under Pablo Acosta and a series of his trafficking predecessors. For a view of the same systems of violence and intimidation in Guadalajara, see Shannon, *Desperados* (n. 139).

155. On the potential for such an outcome in Mexico, see Richard B. Craig, "Mexican Narcotics Traffic: Binational Security Implications," in Mabry, *The Latin American Narcotics Trade*, 29-32 (see n. 124). For the Mexican government's concerns, see the interview with Enrique Alvarez del Castillo in "From Beyond the Border," *New Perspectives Quarterly* 6, no. 2 (Summer 1989).

156. Alan Riding, *Distant Neighbors* (New York: Vintage Books, 1986), 164-65.

157. See, for example, Peter A. Lupsha, "Drug Lords and Narco-corruption: The Players Change but the Game Continues," in Alfred W. McCoy and Alan A. Block, eds., *War on Drugs: Studies in the Failure of U.S. Narcotics Policy* (Boulder, CO: Westview Press, 1992).

158. On the shootout, see: Edward Cody, "Drug Bust Goes Awry in Mexico," *Washington Post*, 29 Nov. 1991; Tim Golden, "Mexican Panel Faults Army in Death of Drug Agents," *New York Times* (international ed.), 7 Dec. 1991; and ibid. In another example, news reports in Nov. 1992 indicated that Manuel Bartlett Diaz—a former education minister who was elected governor of Puebla State in 1992—may have been linked to the killings of a Mexican journalist and U.S. drug enforcement agent Enrique Camarena. Both the journalist and Camarena were reportedly investigating Bartlett's ties to the drug trade. A DEA report linking Bartlett to the murders was obtained by a reporter at the *Mexico City News* who intended to run a story on the charges prior to the gubernatorial elections in which Bartlett was a candidate. According to press reports, executives at the newspaper—including a close friend of Bartlett—ordered the reporter to kill the story. "A Governor's Free Ride?" *Newsweek*, 23 Nov. 1992.

159. Candice Hughes, "Slaying of Drug Agents Touchy Issue in Mexico," *Albuquerque Journal*, 28 Nov. 1991.

160. The family of Jaime ("Don Jaime") Herrera-Nevarez is the economic and political power structure in Durango, and it has not been seriously weakened by U.S. or Mexican law enforcement efforts that have put members of the family in jail on occasion over the years. Originally enriched by traffic in heroin, the Herrera family expanded into cocaine trafficking in response to market demands in the United States. The family is

now linked to Colombian traffickers, through both business ties and marriage. With a network of several thousand relatives and operatives linked in a cartel of interrelated family groups, the Herrera operations stretch from Durango to Chicago, New York, Philadelphia, Boston, Detroit, and Louisville. Interview with Gallagher (see n. 121); Howard Abadinsky, *Organized Crime* (Chicago: Nelson-Hall, 1990), 230-31. Other important trafficking families are the Talavera organization in Juárez-El Paso and the Juan Garcia Abrego family in Brownsville-Matamoros.

161. Richard Craig, "La Campaña Permanente: Mexico's Antidrug Campaign," *Journal of Interamerican Studies and World Affairs* (May 1978):107-33.

162. As noted by Elaine Shannon, Nixon had domestic political reasons not related to the drug trade for getting tough on trafficking. Nixon campaigned in 1968 on a law-and-order ticket, vowing to rein in the "permissiveness" of U.S. society and clean up street crime. Once in office, however, he found himself constrained by the requirements of the federal system, in which decisions about most aspects of crime and punishment are reserved to state and local governments. The administration seized on drug trafficking for its get-tough policies because antinarcotics efforts fell within the responsibilities of the executive branch and had an impact on U.S. street crime. Shannon, *Desperados*, 47 (see n. 139). On Operation Intercept, see Richard B. Craig, "Operation Intercept: The International Politics of Pressure," *Review of Politics* 42, no. 4 (Oct. 1980).

163. According to Samuel I. del Villar, Nixon's Operation Intercept was designed in part to force Mexico to use chemicals to destroy marijuana and poppy crops. Nixon aide G. Gordon Liddy, one of those involved in implementing the plan and a culprit in the Watergate scandal, was straightforward about the coercive intentions of the operation: "It was an exercise in international extortion, pure and simple and effective, designed to bend Mexico to our will. We figured Mexico could hold out for a month; in fact, they caved in after two weeks, and we got what we wanted." Quoted in del Villar, "The Illicit U.S.-Mexico Drug Market," 200 (see n. 136).

164. Richard Craig, "Operation Condor: Mexico's Antidrug Campaign Enters a New Era," *Journal of Inter-American Studies and World Affairs* (1980), 345, 360.

165. See the summary of these programs in *Drug Control* (n. 139). Also see ibid.

166. Craig, "Operation Condor" (see n. 164).

167. For good descriptions of the extent of corruption during the mid-1980s, see Shannon, *Desperados* (n. 139).

168. Agency for International Development, *U.S. Overseas Loans and Grants and Assistance from International Organizations* (Washington, DC, various years).

169. Interviews with Elizabeth Carroll, U.S. Department of State, Bureau of International Narcotics Matters, 3 Sept. 1992 and 29 July 1993.

170. Interview with Carroll, 29 July 1993 (ibid.).

171. Craig, "Mexican Narcotics Traffic," 38 (see n. 155).

172. See the assessments of the U.S.-Mexico drug policy relationship in ibid. and in del Villar, "The Illicit U.S.-Mexico Drug Market" (n. 136); del Villar, "Rethinking Hemispheric Antinarcotics Strategy and Security" (n. 138); and Richard Craig, "U.S. Narcotics Policy toward Mexico: Consequences for the Bilateral Relationship," in Guadalupe González and Marta Tienda, eds., *The Drug Connection in U.S.-Mexican Relations* (San Diego: Center for U.S.-Mexican Studies, 1989).

173. Each of these initiatives was known as Operation Intercept. The first was designed to pressure Mexico into stepping up its eradication and interdiction activities. The second was intended to push Mexico into pursuing and prosecuting the murderers of U.S. drug enforcement agent Enrique Camarena.

174. Office of National Drug Control Policy, *National Drug Control Strategy* (Washington, DC: Government Printing Office, Feb. 1991), 82.

175. *Memorandum of Justification for Presidential Determination Regarding the Drawdown of Defense Articles and Services for Mexico* (Washington, DC: U.S. Department of State, 8 Nov. 1991).

176. As of 1990, thirty-nine DEA special agents and three DEA intelligence analysts were stationed in Mexico. DEA offices are located in Mexico City, Guadalajara, Hermosillo, Mazatlán, Merida, and Monterrey. *Mexico: A Country Profile* (Washington, DC: Drug Enforcement Administration, Dec. 1991).

177. Shannon, *Desperados*, 123 (see n. 139).

178. The available sources on these topics are manifold. For a detailed look at the Camarena case and DEA in Mexico during the early and mid-1980s, see ibid. A good example of Mexico bashing in response to a variety of drug-related and other "incidents" is recorded in the so-called Helms hearings, a set of hearings held in 1986 before the U.S. Senate Subcommittee on Western Hemisphere Affairs. The subcommittee is chaired by Sen. Jesse Helms, a sharp critic of the Mexican government. Hearings before the U.S. Senate Subcommittee on Western Hemisphere Affairs of the Committee on Foreign Relations, *Situation in Mexico*, 99th Cong., 2nd sess., 13 May, 17 and 26 June 1986. Also see hearing before the U.S. House of Representatives Select Committee on Narcotics Abuse and Control, *U.S. Narcotics Control Efforts in Mexico and on the Southwest Border*, 99th Cong., 2nd. sess., 22 July 1986. On the satellite controversy, see Douglas Jehl and Doyle McManus, "Mexico Assails U.S. Figures on Producing Pot," *Los Angeles Times*, 1 March 1990, and "Mexico Angry at U.S. over Use of Satellite," *New York Times*, 17 March 1990.

179. Not just a set of cowboy actions, the abductions of the Camarena conspirators also sprang from real human frustration. DEA agents investigating Camarena's disappearance and his subsequent murder found their legitimate efforts repeatedly blocked by Mexican officials. From the DEA perspective, Camarena had not just been killed in the line of duty, as Mexican critics insisted. The brutality of the murder went beyond what was necessary just to get the agent out of the way. Camarena was tortured for some thirty hours. He was beaten with pipes and fists, kicked, and he was sodomized with objects. His murderers finished him off by driving a tire iron through his skull. Collecting evidence, DEA agents listened repeatedly to tapes made by the traffickers of Camarena's last hours. Intended to document the interrogation so that the conspirators could determine how much was known of their operations and protectors in Mexico, the tapes also recorded the bitterly slow death of the agent. Worse, informants told the DEA that Camarena was kept alive longer than naturally possible by Humberto Alvarez Macháin, a Guadalajara physician. The informants said that Alvarez injected Camarena with the stimulant lidocaine to keep his heart from failing until the traffickers had all their questions answered. The failure of the Mexican government to pursue a timely and thorough investigation of the murder—one that would look into the full reach of the conspiracy—reinforced DEA inclinations to act unilaterally. Although this explanation does not justify the violation of Mexican territory, the justice and human rights concerns raised by the murder and its aftermath demonstrate the complicated nature of the DEA abductions. But the fact that the United States could get away with these actions, Mexican opposition notwithstanding, clearly illustrates the asymmetry between the two countries.

Adding another twist to this grim account, when Alvarez was brought to trial in the United States, a district judge acquitted him after the prosecution had rested its case. The judge found that the prosecution had produced insufficient evidence to convict Alvarez and dismissed the case before the decision was even turned over to the jury. Linda Deutsch, "Judge Clears Mexican Doctor in Camarena Slaying," *Albuquerque Journal*, 15 Dec. 1992. Later newspaper reports indicated that the DEA had been told by an informant two months before the trial that *another* doctor had administered the drugs to keep Camarena alive. The DEA did not even tell the prosecution about this information until well into the trial, and the information was not given to the judge until immediately before his decision to clear Alvarez. Linda Deutsch, "Informant Blames Other Doctor in Camarena Death," *Albuquerque Journal*, 17 Dec. 1992.

180. Macháin was the physician who allegedly prolonged Camarena's life with drugs so that his torturers could finish their interrogation. Mexico had made no effort to indict him for his participation in the crime.

181. Interview with Gallagher (see n. 121).

182. For a brief but informative overview of the pitfalls of a drug-control strategy that relies primarily on enforcement and interdiction, see Peter Reuter, *Can the Borders Be Sealed?* (Santa Monica, CA: Rand Corporation, Aug. 1988).

183. Juan Garcia, *Operation Wetback* (Tucson: University of Arizona Press, 1980), 175.

184. The best overview of border militarization under the Carter, Reagan, and Bush administrations is Timothy J. Dunn, *The Militarization of the U.S.-Mexico Border, 1978-1992: Low Intensity Conflict Doctrine Comes Home* (Austin, TX: Center for Mexican-American Studies, forthcoming). Much of the discussion in this section draws on Dunn's excellent work.

185. Interview with Timothy Dunn, 11 Nov. 1992.

186. According to James Olech, the Border Patrol's chief of Management Support, 10 percent to 50 percent of the agents carry semiautomatic pistols. Cited in Americas Watch, *Human Rights in Mexico: A Policy of Impunity* (New York, June 1990), 86.

187. For example, Congress amended the Posse Comitatus Act, a law dating from 1878 that restricts military involvement in domestic law enforcement activities. The 1981 revisions clarified and expanded the ways the military could contribute to civilian law enforcement operations. The amended law permitted the armed forces to share information, equipment, and facilities with civilian law enforcement agencies, and to provide them with training and the personnel to operate and maintain equipment lent to them by the military.

188. The 1986 Omnibus Drug Control Act required the military to become more active in interdiction efforts, and the 1989 Defense Authorization Act designated the Department of Defense the lead agency for detecting and monitoring aerial and maritime transport of illegal drugs.

189. Statement of James E. Bowen, senior tactical coordinator of Operation Alliance, in a hearing before the U.S. Senate Committee on Appropriations, *Federal, State, and Local Drug Enforcement and Interdiction Efforts along the Southwest Border*, 100th Cong., 2nd sess., 1989.

190. See the extensive coverage of these services and their importance to U.S. border control in Dunn, *Militarization of the U.S.-Mexico Border* (n. 184).

191. Lt. Col. John Kiser, quoted in Ruben Hernandez, "Marines Aid Border Agents," *Tucson Citizen*, 31 Aug. 1992.

192. Ibid.

193. During the confrontation the marines launched an illumination flare into the night sky. When the flare fell to earth, it ignited a fire that burned three hundred acres of national forest land. Moreover, it turned out that local law enforcement officials had not been informed that Marines were patrolling in their jurisdiction. Miriam Davidson, "Militarizing the Mexican Border," *The Nation*, 1 April 1991. So far this has been the only incident in which military forces have engaged in a shootout while on these operations, but when they are in the field, they operate on rules of engagement that authorize them to shoot to kill if they or their civilian companions are endangered.

194. Hernandez, "Marines Aid Border Agents" (see n. 191).

195. Interview with Ruben Hernandez, *Tucson Citizen*, 12 Nov. 1992.

196. Many of these efforts, in fact, have been strongly criticized for being disorganized, badly coordinated, understaffed, inefficient, and ineffective. See, for instance, Com-

mittee on Government Operations, *Operation Alliance: Drug Interdiction on the Southwest Border* (Washington, DC: Government Printing Office, 1988), and *Drug Interdiction: Operation Harvest: A National Guard-Customs Anti-Smuggling Effort* (Washington, DC: General Accounting Office, June 1988).

197. On the Alien Border Control Committee and other border emergency contingency plans, see Dunn, *Militarization of the U.S.-Mexico Border*, 67-71 (n. 184).

198. Ibid., 198.

199. Davidson, "Militarizing the Mexican Border" (see n. 193).

200. Statement before Subcommittee on Human Rights, 18 June 1990.

201. For a valuable, although dated, book-length overview of the border economy, see Niles Hansen, *The Border Economy: Regional Development in the Southwest* (Austin: University of Texas Press, 1981).

202. Quoted in Bruce Stokes, "Boom at the Border," *National Journal*, 29 July 1989. Saxod has since become director of the Border Progress Foundation.

203. Maquiladoras in the textile industry must be 51 percent Mexican-owned. The textile industry is subject to export quotas under the Multilateral Fibre Agreement, to which both the United States and Mexico are parties.

204. Despite the constitutional prohibition against foreign ownership of any land within 62.5 miles (a hundred kilometers) of the border, foreign businesses gain the ownership rights they want through *fideicomisos*, which are thirty-year trusts that make Mexican banks the legal owner of land but grant foreign businesses primary use of the property. If a new foreign investment law President Salinas plans to submit to Congress early in 1993 passes, any company incorporated in Mexico will reportedly be able to purchase land in Mexico's forbidden border zone. If true, maquilas would no longer need *fideicomisos*.

205. Quoted in *Business Mexico*, Feb. 1986.

206. Vast literature exists on the maquiladoras. Probably the best source of data, analysis, and historic detail is Leslie Sklair, *Assembling for Development: The Maquila Industry in Mexico and the United States* (Winchester, MA: Unwin Hyman, 1989). Other valuable sources include Joseph Grunwald and Kenneth Flamm, eds., *The Global Factory: Foreign Assembly in International Trade* (Washington, DC: Brookings, 1985), and *The Use and Economic Impact of TSUS Items 806.30 and 807.00* (Washington, DC: U.S. International Trade Commission, 1988).

207. Of the 2,042 maquiladoras operating in 1992, 12 percent are not located in the six Mexican border states and another 9 percent are located a little more than twelve miles (twenty kilometers) from the border within the border states. American Chamber of Commerce, *Maquiladora Newsletter*, 3rd. q. (1992). According to Sklair, the main differences between border and nonborder maquilas are lower wages, less infrastructure, and the greater propensity of some nonborder maquilas to make local purchases. Sklair, *Assembling for Development* (ibid.).

208. Data from Mexico's National Institute of Statistics, Geography, and Information, (INEGI) and the Ministry of Programming and Budget (SPP), cited in Business International Corp., *Succeeding in the New Mexico: Corporate Strategy, Globalization and the Free Trade Agreement* (New York, 1991), 198. Making the increase in value added per employee even more impressive is the fact that real wages were lower in 1989 than in 1983. The wage rate is relevant because wages make up a large portion of value added in the maquiladoras.

209. Francisco Lara Valencia, "La fuerza de trabajo en la industria maquiladora de la región fronteriza de Sonora: Características socioeconómicas y transición ocupacional," paper prepared for the XV Simposio de Historia y Antropología de Sonora, Hermosillo, Sonora, 21-24 Feb. 1990, 6.

210. Data from SECOFI cited in *La Jornada*, 14 Dec. 1992.

211. Fixed direct investment in the maquiladoras has been estimated at $5 billion. Leslie Sklair, *The Maquiladoras: Present Status, Future Potential*, study submitted to the U.S. Office of Technology Assessment (Dec. 1991). This amount implies average annual investment of more than $600 million assuming standard depreciation rates. It is impossible to know how much of the direct investment is recorded in Mexico, since a great deal of the equipment used in maquilas is leased from U.S.-based parent companies. In such cases the investment dollars stay in the United States.

212. Patricia A. Wilson, "The New Maquiladoras: Flexible Production in Low Wage Regions," in Khostrow Fatemi, ed., *Maquiladoras: Economic Problem or Solution?* (New York: Praeger, 1990). For the increasing productivity of maquila workers see Bernardo González-Aréchiga and José Carlos Ramiréz, "Productividad sin distribución: Cambio tecnológico en la industria maquiladora Mexicana (1980-86)," *Frontera Norte* 1, no. 1 (Jan.-June 1989).

213. See, for example, Roberto A. Sánchez, "Condiciones de vida de los trabajadores de la maquiladora en Tijuana y Nogales," *Frontera Norte* 4, no. 2 (July-Dec. 1990). The average total compensation cost per worker-hour in Mexican manufacturing as a whole was $2.17 in 1991. For the maquiladora sector by itself the figure was $1.55. These amounts reflect direct wages, such benefits as annual bonuses, vacations, and subsidized meals, and payroll taxes. From *International Comparisons of Hourly Compensation Costs for Production Workers in Manufacturing, 1991*, Report 825 (Washington, DC: U.S. Department of Labor, Bureau of Labor Statistics, June 1992), and from unpublished data compiled by the Bureau of Labor Statistics.

214. *Twin Plant News*, Jan. 1987.

215. See, for example, U.S. Congress, Office of Technology Assessment, *U.S.-Mexico Trade: Pulling Together or Pulling Apart?* ITE-545 (Washington, DC: Government Printing Office, Oct. 1992), 81; G.W. Lucker, "The Hidden Costs of Worker Turnover: A Case Study in the Maquiladora Industry," *Journal of Borderlands Studies* 2 (1987); and Sklair, *Assembling for Development*, 179 (n. 206).

216. Quoted in Harley Shaiken, "The Auto and Electronics Sectors in U.S.-Mexico Trade and Investment," study submitted to the U.S. Office of Technology Assessment (Washington, DC: May 1992), 44-45.

217. Beginning in the late 1980s some researchers argued that the composition of maquiladoras was shifting toward increasingly high-technology industries, and that maquiladoras were adopting new forms of work organization and greater training. See: Jorge Carrillo, "Transformaciones en la industria maquiladora de exportación," in Bernardo González-Aréchiga and Rocío Barajas Escamilla, eds., *Las maquiladoras: Ajuste estructural y desarrollo regional* (Tijuana: COLEF and Fundación Friedrich Ebert, 1989); and Leonard Mertens and Laura Palomares, "El surgimiento de un nuevo tipo de trabajador en la industria de alta tecnología: El caso electrónico," in Estela Gutiérrez, ed., *Testimonios de la crisis I* (Mexico, D.F.: Siglo XXI, 1988).

   Many of these studies confused high-technology sectors, like electronics, with high-technology production processes. Furthermore, even where high-technology production processes were used, training requirements for line workers were still minimal, with training focused on plant technicians. One report that asserts that "training occupies a central place within the managerial strategies in the maquiladora plants" found nevertheless that only 25 percent of the plants surveyed offered technical training programs in the three years prior to the study. Jorge Carrillo, *Mercados de trabajo en la industria maquiladora de exportación* (Mexico: COLEF and STPS, 1991). For further exploration of these issues, see Wilson, "The New Maquiladoras," in Fatemi, *Maquiladoras* (n. 212); Harley Shaiken and Harry Browne, "Japanese Work Organization in Mexico," in Gabriel Székely, ed., *Manufacturing across Borders and Oceans: Japan, the United States, and Mexico* (San Diego: Center for U.S.-Mexican Studies, 1991); and

Cathryn L. Thorup, ed., *The United States and Mexico: Face to Face with New Technology* (New Brunswick, ME: Transaction Books, 1987).

218. There are many factors explaining this low level of domestic supply, including the failure of the government to mandate a local-supply percentage, the low quality and inefficiency of many Mexican producers, and the unwillingness of Mexican industries to retool to meet the needs of firms that may withdraw their investment at any time. On the border, there is also the fact that isolation from the Mexican interior and close commercial relations with the U.S. side (including a history of free trade) have discouraged the development of local industry.

219. Numerous studies have addressed Mexico's failure to establish linkages between its maquila sector and its domestic economy. One important look at this question is Joseph Grunwald, "Opportunity Missed: Mexico and Maquiladoras," *Brookings Review* (Winter 1990-91).

220. For more on the "triple alliance," see Leslie Sklair, "The Maquila Industry and the Creation of a Transnational Capitalist Class in the United States-Mexico Border Region," in Herzog, *Changing Boundaries*, 69-88 (n. 22).

221. What little serious labor organizing there is in the maquilas has occurred in the Rio Grande Valley, mainly in Matamoros. See Edward J. Williams, "Attitudes and Strategies Inhibiting the Unionization of the Maquiladora Industry: Government, Industry, Unions, and Workers," *Journal of Borderland Studies* 6, no. 2, and Edward J. Williams and John T. Passé-Smith, *The Unionization of the Maquiladora Industry: The Tamaulipan Case in National Context* (San Diego: Institute for Regional Studies of the Californias, San Diego State University, 1992).

222. Peter Baird and Ed McCaughn, "Hit and Run: U.S. Runaway Shops on the Mexican Border," *Report on the Americas* (July-Aug. 1975).

223. Talli Nauman, "Maquiladoras Thrive Despite Doubts," *El Financiero International*, 9 Nov. 1992, and Brad Stratton, "Learning English Is Not Enough," *Quality Progress*, Jan. 1989.

224. In 1988, 44 percent of the maquilas and 75 percent of the jobs were found in specialized industrial parks for the maquila sector. Thomas P. Lee, ed., *In-bond Industry/Industria Maquiladora* (Mexico, D.F.: Administración y Servicios Internacionales, 1988).

225. Mexican capitalists and professionals also play an important role in the maquila sector mainly by setting up industrial parks, providing services, and acting as subcontractors. See Alejandra Salas-Porras, "Maquiladoras y burguesía regional," *El Cotidiano*, Edición Especial, 1987.

226. Sklair, *Assembling for Development*, 235 (see n. 206).

227. The Programa Nacional Fronterizo (PRONAF) was established by President López Mateos in 1961 to promote social and economic development and make the border a "window on Mexico." The program was short-lived and not well-funded, but it did result in the construction of the PRONAF tourist centers in Juárez and Tijuana.

228. This point is made well by Sklair, who observed, "The great hopes on which the maquila strategy rests, namely that Mexico could supply substantial quantities of material inputs to the maquila industry, backward linkages, and that it could derive massive, virtually free technology spinoffs and genuine technology transfers, have not been realized." This was based on a faulty understanding of the ideology and practice of production sharing, according to Sklair, *Assembling for Development*, 227 (see n. 206). Also see Joseph Grunwald, "U.S.-Mexican Production Sharing in World Perspective," in Paul Ganster, ed., *The Maquiladora Program in Trinational Perspective: Mexico, Japan, and the United States* (San Diego: Institute for Regional Studies of the Californias, San Diego State University, 1987).

229. For analysis of why Mexico has failed to increase domestic linkages and use the maquila sector to spur broader industrialization see Patricia A. Wilson, "The Global As-

sembly Industry: Maquiladoras in International Perspective," Community and Regional Working Paper Series, no. 10 (Austin: University of Texas, July 1989), and Grunwald, "Opportunity Missed" (n. 219).

230. See Sklair, *The Maquiladoras*, 16 (see n. 211).

231. Among such companies are Ansell International of Columbus, Ohio, a surgical glove manufacturer, and two producers of electronic components, Pike Engineering and Valor Electronics. *Wall Street Journal*, 14 Jan. 1991.

232. NAFTA requires Mexico to phase out the heart of the Border Industrialization Program—its duty-free provisions—by 1 Jan. 2001. "NAFTA to End Maquila Program," *El Financiero International*, 7 Sept. 1992.

233. Auto parts are subject to the general 60 percent regional-content rule under NAFTA, but they are affected indirectly by the rule of origin governing automobiles. In calculating the local content of autos, NAFTA requires that the foreign-origin portion of auto parts be considered as foreign content in the finished car, even when the parts themselves pass the regional-content test. In all other industries such foreign content in components may be "rolled up" and considered as local content if the component meets the applicable rule of origin. Medium- and large-size televisions must contain North American-made picture tubes in addition to the standard regional content to qualify for duty-free status, and computers must contain a regionally produced motherboard. The restrictions on textiles and apparel are probably the most onerous of all. Local content must be at least 80 percent, and not only the fabric used to make the apparel but even the yarn used to make the fabric must be sourced from the United States, Mexico, or Canada. See James Bovard, "NAFTA's Protectionist Bent," *Wall Street Journal*, 31 July 1992; Douglas Karmin, "Rules of Origin and the North American Free Trade Agreement," *CRS Report for Congress*, 21 Aug. 1992; and *Rules of Origin Issues Related to NAFTA and the North American Automotive Industry*, USITC Publication 2460 (Washington, DC: U.S. International Trade Commission, Nov. 1991).

234. "Wharton Econometrics Projects High Growth for Maquiladora Industry, 1993-1997," *La Jornada*, 3 Dec. 1992.

235. Eduardo Zepeda Miramontes, "NAFTA and Industrialization on the Northern Border," in Ganster and Valenciano, *The Mexican-U.S. Border Region*, 45 (see n. 68).

236. Advertisements in *Twin Plant News*, as cited by Jim Dougherty, *McBorderland USA: The Maquiladora Industry and the Selling of El Paso, Texas and Ciudad Juárez, Mexico*, working paper series (Buffalo: University of Buffalo, Baldy Center for Law and Social Policy, 1992), 7.

237. Interview with Sam Drake, El Paso Industrial Development Corporation, 23 July 1992.

238. A study of forty-three education centers along the border found that over half had maquila-related courses and many of the teachers were maquila staff. Carrillo, *Mercados de Trabajo*, cited in Sklair, *The Maquiladoras*, 21 (see n. 211).

239. John F. Garmon, "The Maquiladora Colleges," *Twin Plant News*, Aug. 1990. Garmon is dean of Occupational Technical Education at Texas Southmost College.

240. Interview with Mike Roark, 28 Oct. 1992.

241. "Back to School: Community Colleges Offer Specialized Maquila Education," *Maquila Magazine*, Sept. 1990.

242. Brad Cooper, "Becoming Part of the Solution," *Maquila Magazine*, Oct. 1991.

243. Interview with Erin Ross, IM[3]'s director of communications, 30 Oct. 1992.

244. Ken W. Chapman, "UTEP Transfers Technology," *Twin Plant News*, May 1992.

245. One of the most prominent critics of this partnership between academia and maquilas has been the AFL-CIO's Victor Muñoz, former chairperson of the El Paso Central Labor Council. One of the first published accounts of this partnership is Dougherty, *McBorderland USA* (see n. 236). Among the Juárez-based maquilas directly assisted by IM[3]

and MVAL that moved to Mexico after closing down operations in the United States are Johnson & Johnson, Thompson Consumer Electronics, Advance Transformer, Baxter Health Care, Delco Products (a division of GM), Honeywell, and Ford Motor Company.

246. Dr. Richard Sprinkle, "An Investigation of the Employment Linkage between Cd. Juárez and El Paso" (El Paso: University of Texas-El Paso, 1986).

247. See Sklair, *Assembling for Development*, 109-10, 182-83 (n. 206). Sklair notes that "the direct causal connection between Juárez maquilas and El Paso jobs must remain a statistical artifact within the Link methodology." It is interesting to note that the Border Trade Alliance was established in 1987 as an outgrowth of a partnership of industry, border governments, and academics to promote the concept of maquila-based development. Initially, the campaign was a response to charges by the AFL-CIO and some members of Congress that the Department of Commerce was directly facilitating the growth of the maquila sector—and hence the number of runaway plants. The position papers prepared in the late 1980s by Michie and others purporting to demonstrate the benefits of the maquila sector to the U.S. borderlands were part of a major lobbying effort in Washington by the Border Trade Alliance.

248. Interview with Donald Michie in *San Francisco Chronicle*, 29 Feb. 1988. See Sklair, *Assembling for Development*, 185-86 (n. 206), for further analysis of the suspect nature of Michie's data.

249. Interview with Donald Michie, 10 Nov. 1992.

250. *Paso del Norte Regional Economy: Socioeconomic Profile* (El Paso: Institute for Manufacturing and Materials Management, Aug. 1991), iv.

251. Ibid., 3.

252. Harry Browne and Beth Sims, *Runaway America: U.S. Jobs and Factories on the Move* (Albuquerque: Resource Center Press, 1993).

253. See Raúl Fernández, *The United States-Mexico Border* (Notre Dame: Notre Dame Press, 1977).

254. Border cities are not alone in their dependence on Mexican trade and visitors. The state of Texas, for example, does more business with Mexico than does any other state—30 percent of its exports go to Mexico. It used to be that petroleum equipment formed the overwhelming bulk of these exports, but Mexico is now importing a much broader variety of goods, including chemical, paper, and metal products as well as an increasing quantity of foodstuffs. *Business Mexico*, Sept. 1990.

255. See *The Impact of Increased United States-Mexico Trade on Southwest Border Development* (Washington, DC: U.S. International Trade Commission, Nov. 1986). There are no region-wide studies of the percentage impact of purchases by Mexican nationals, but most researchers and observers reported a dramatic decline after the 1982 devaluation, much of which has subsequently been recouped.

256. Study by E. George, "Impact of the Maquilas on Manpower Development and Economic Growth on the U.S./Mexico Border" (El Paso: University of Texas-El Paso, 1986), cited in Sklair, *The Maquiladoras*, 19 (see n. 211).

257. See Valencia, "La fuerza de trabajo" (n. 209). According to Valencia, maquila production workers in Nogales spend $67 of their wages in the United States on food and clothing each month.

258. Sklair, *The Maquiladoras*, 19 (see n. 211).

259. Interview with Henry King, associate director of Center for Enterprise Development Advancement Research and Support, 4 Nov. 1992.

260. Yazmin Venegas Peralta, "Retorno a la economía de Estados Unidos," *El Financiero*, 4 Dec. 1990.

261. *The Impact of Increased United States-Mexico Trade*, 17-20 (see n. 255). In Dec. 1984 Laredo and McAllen had the highest and second highest unemployment rates in the United States.

262. J. Williams, "Mexicans Shopping in Texas Add to Profits of Border Malls," *Washington Post*, 7 Jan. 1990.

263. According to estimates by the Banco Nacional de Mexico, cited in *Washington Post*, 7 Jan. 1990.

264. For an entertaining account of the new Nogales see Jim Henderson, "Border Boom Town," *American Way*, 1 Nov. 1990.

265. "Brothels Bloom in Nuevo Laredo," *Herald Post*, 16 Oct. 1990.

266. P.R. Casner and L.G. Guerra, "Purchasing Prescription Medication in Mexico," *Western Journal of Medicine* (1 May 1992).

267. Jan Gilbreath, "Financing Environmental and Infrastructure Needs on the Texas-Mexico Border: Will the Mexican-U.S. Integrated Border Plan Help?" *Journal of Environment and Development* 1, no. 1 (Summer 1992).

268. Between 1987 and 1990 northbound border truck traffic increased more than 40 percent, but customs services have not been able to keep up with this new pace. During the same period the Customs Service increased the number of inspectors by just 12 percent. *U.S.-Mexico Trade: Concerns about the Adequacy of Border Infrastructure* (Washington, DC: General Accounting Office, May 1991), 13.

269. See *Integrated Environmental Plan for the Mexican-U.S. Border Area* (Washington, DC: Environmental Protection Agency and SEDUE, 1992).

270. The GAO's report *U.S.-Mexico Trade* (n. 268), for example, addresses only the need for better customs and transportation infrastructure, saying nothing about social services.

271. Cited in David Maraniss, "On Both Sides of the Border, Laredo's Alienation Runs Deep," *Washington Post*, 29 June 1986.

272. See Gilbreath, "Financing Environmental and Infrastructure Needs," 166-67 (n. 267), and Jan Gilbreath Rich, *Planning the Border's Future: The Mexican-U.S. Integrated Border Environmental Plan*, U.S.-Mexican Occasional Paper No. 1, (Austin: Lyndon B. Johnson School of Public Affairs, University of Texas at Austin, March 1992), 31.

273. Eduardo Zepeda Miramontes, *La infraestructura en la frontera norte y el proceso de liberalización comercial* (Tijuana: COLEF, 1992).

274. Keith Bradsher, "Trade Accord at Stake, U.S. Weighs a Border Bond Issue," *New York Times*, 29 July 1993, and Martin Crutsinger, "Free Trade," *Associated Press*, 29 July 1993.

275. A good overview of Mexico's centralized tax system is Ted Bardacke, "Reforms Aside, Hacienda Still Controls the Purse Strings," *El Financiero International*, 14 Dec. 1992.

276. Quoted in George Baker, "Who's Afraid of the FTA?" in Ganster and Valenciano, *The Mexican-U.S. Border Region*, 17 (see n. 68).

277. George Baker, "Mexican Labor Is Not Cheap," *Rio Bravo: A Journal of Research and Opinion* 1, no. 1 (Oct. 1991).

278. Some maquiladora operators declare minimal net income in Mexico to avoid the slight chance of an audit by the Ministry of Finance. Two experts on maquila accounting issues recommend that "transfer prices should be established which will result in Mexican taxable income equal to about 1 percent or 2 percent of sales." Cheryl D. Hein and Neal R. VanZante, "Maquiladoras: Should U.S. Companies Run for the Border?" *The CPA Journal*, Oct. 91.

279. The tax—30 percent of total wages prorated for work time spent in Mexico—was to apply to anyone working fifteen days or more in the country during a given year. After revision to accommodate maquiladora protests, the tax rate remained the same but

was applied only to persons working more than 183 days in country. Diane Lindquist, "Maquiladora Operators Gain Break on New Tax," *San Diego Union-Tribune*, 7 May 1992, C1, and American Chamber of Commerce/Mexico, "Mexico Adjusts its Taxation—Non-Residents Now Included," *Review of Trade and Industry*, 2nd. q. (1992), 4-8.

280. Study cited ibid., 170.

281. Some firms have, however, benefited from INFONAVIT funds used by official unions to create housing for maquila workers.

282. Quoted in David Clark Scott, "Mexico's Border Industry Faces Housing Crisis," *Christian Science Monitor*, 28 June 1991.

283. This was the leading theme of the widely touted Border Environmental Infrastructure Colloquy, sponsored by the U.S. Environmental Protection Agency and Mexico's SEDESOL, in Santa Fe, NM, 26 June 1992. Also see Cooper, "Becoming Part of the Solution" (n. 242).

284. One of the leading advocates is border promoter Charlie Crowder, who told one reporter, "If we want to be the problem, we can be. All we've got to do is build some factories. And we can take an impossible paralysis of social infrastructure and human misery, and contribute to it. But it is not good business." Sandy Tolan, "The Border Boom: Hope and Heartbreak," *New York Times Magazine*, 1 July 1990.

285. Quoted in Stokes, "Boom at the Border" (see n. 202).

Selected Border Organizations

American Friends Service Committee (AFSC)
1501 Cherry St.
Philadelphia, PA 19102
Phone: (215) 241-7132
Fax: (215) 241-7275
Contact: Primitivo Rodriguez, National Director, U.S.-Mexico Border Program

American Friends Service Committee (AFSC)
U.S.-Mexico Border Program
PO Box 126147
San Diego, CA 92112
Phone: (619) 233-4114
Fax: (619) 233-6247
Contact: Roberto Martínez, Director

American Friends Service Committee (AFSC)
Immigration Law Enforcement Monitoring Project (ILEMP)
515 Allen Parkway
Houston, TX 77019
Phone: (713) 524-5428
Fax: (713) 524-8183
Contact: Maria Jimenez, Project Director

Border Research Institute
New Mexico State University
4200 Research Dr.
Las Cruces, NM 88003
Phone: (505) 646-3524
Fax: (505) 646-5474
Contact: Maria Telles-McGeagh, Director

Center for Inter-American and Border Studies (CIABS)
University of Texas at El Paso (UTEP)
Administration Bldg. #320
El Paso, TX 79968
Phone: (915) 747-5196
Fax: (915) 747-5574
Contact: Samuel Schmidt

Coalition for Justice in the Maquiladoras (CJM)
3120 W. Ashby
San Antonio, TX 78228
Phone: (210) 732-8957
Fax: (210) 732-8324
Contact: Susan Mika

Colegio de la Frontera Norte (COLEF)
Blvd. Abelardo L. Rodríguez 21
Zona del Río
Tijuana, B.C. 22320
Phone: (66) 30-04-11
Fax: (66) 30-00-50
U.S. mailing address: PO Box "L", Chula Vista, CA 92912
Contact: Dr. Jorge Carrillo V., Academic General Director

Colegio de la Frontera Norte–Ciudad Juárez
Av. Campestre 100
Campestre Juárez
Ciudad Juárez, Chih. 32460
Phone: (16) 17-57-02
Fax: (16) 17-89-58
U.S. mailing address: PO Box 1385, El Paso, TX 79948
Contact: Eduardo Barrera

Colegio de la Frontera Norte–Matamoros
Av. Alvaro Obregón 12
Edif. Rebeca #315, Col. Jardín
Matamoros, Tamps.
Phone/fax: (891) 3-45-59
U.S. mailing address: PO Box 2136, Brownsville, TX 78522
Contact: Cirila Quintero Ramírez

Colegio de la Frontera Norte–Mexicali
Calafia e Independencia 1096 #1
Centro Cívico
Mexicali, B.C. 21000
Phone: (65) 57-53-41
Fax: (65) 57-25-89
U.S. mailing address: PO Box 8220, Calexico, CA 92231
Contact: Jesús Adolfo Román Calleros, Regional Director of the Dirección
  Regional del Noroeste, or Francisco A. Bernal Rodríguez

Colegio de la Frontera Norte–Monterrey
Bolivia 313, Col. Vista Hermosa
Monterrey, N.L. 64620
Phone: (83) 48-57-03
Contact: Victor Zúñiga, Regional Director of the Dirección Regional de Noreste

Colegio de la Frontera Norte–Nogales
Calle Campodónico 303, Col. Granja
Nogales, Son. 84065
Phone: (631) 3-04-26
Fax: (631) 3-21-85
U.S. mailing address: PO Box 3048, Nogales, AZ 85628
Contact: Franciso Lara Valencia, Coordinator, or Irasema Coronado

Colegio de la Frontera Norte–Nuevo Laredo
Chihuahua 2509, Col. Guerrero
Nuevo Laredo, Tamps. 88240
Phone: (871) 5-12-63
Fax: (871) 5-82-63
U.S. mailing address: PO Box 6415, Laredo, TX 78042
Contact: Manuel Ceballos Ramírez, Coordinator

Colegio de la Frontera Norte–Piedras Negras
Progreso y Hacienda 503, Col. Burocratas
Piedras Negras, Coah. 26020
Phone: (878) 2-53-00
Fax: (878) 2-50-20
U.S. mailing address: PO Box 7235, Eagle Pass, TX 78853
Contact: Camilo Contreras Delgado or Francisco René Vidaurrázaga O.

Colegio de Sonora
Av. Obregón 54
Col. Centro
Hermosillo, Son. 83000
Phone: (62) 12-50-21/65-51
Fax: (62) 12-00-15
Contact: Catalina A. Denman, Director

International Transboundary Resource Center (CIRT)
University of New Mexico Law School
1117 Stanford NE
Albuquerque, NM 87131
Phone: (505) 277-4820
Contact: Albert E. Utton, Director

Institute for Regional Studies of the Californias (IRSC)
San Diego State University
San Diego, CA 92182-0435
Phone: (619) 594-5423
Fax: (619) 594-5474
Contact: Paul Ganster

Journal of Borderlands Studies
Department of Economics
Box 30001
New Mexico State University
Las Cruces, NM 88003
Phone: (505) 646-2113/3113
Contact: James T. Peach

Seminario Permanente de Estudios Chicanos y de Fronteras
Dirección de Etnología y Antropología Social (DEAS)
Instituto Nacional de Antropología e Historia (INAH)
Plaza del Carmen 4 y 6
Col. San Angel
México, D.F. 01000
Phone: (5) 5-50-80-43/05-32
Fax: (5) 6-59-48-37
Contact: Juan Manuel Sandoval, General Coordinator

Texas Industrial Areas Foundation Network
1106 W. Clayton Lane #120 W
Austin, TX 78723
Phone: (512) 459-6551
Fax: (512) 459-6558
Contact: Dell Watson

Udall Center for Studies in Public Policy
University of Arizona
803/811 E. 1st St.
Tucson, AZ 85719
Phone: (602) 621-7189
Fax: (602) 621-9234
Contact: Robert G. Varady, Associate Director

U.S.-Mexican Policy Studies Program
L.B. Johnson School of Public Affairs
University of Texas at Austin
PO Box 7819
Austin, TX 78713-7819
Phone: (512) 471-1835
Fax: (512) 471-8951
Contact: Sidney Weintraub

About the Authors

Tom Barry has been a senior analyst at the Inter-Hemispheric Education Resource Center since its founding in 1979. He is a co-author of *The Great Divide: The Challenge of U.S.-Mexico Relations in the 1990s* (Grove Press, forthcoming) and is the author or co-author of all the books in the Resource Center's *Country Guide* series. He is the author of *Central America Inside Out* (Grove Weidenfeld, 1991), co-author of *Feeding the Crisis* (University of Nebraska Press, 1991), and author of *Roots of Rebellion* (South End Press, 1986).

Harry Browne is a research associate at the Inter-Hemispheric Education Resource Center. He is a co-author of *The Great Divide: The Challenge of U.S.-Mexico Relations in the 1990s* and of *Runaway America: U.S. Jobs and Factories on the Move* (Resource Center Press, 1993). He received his Master's of Pacific International Affairs from the Graduate School of International Relations and Pacific Studies at the University of California, San Diego.

Beth Sims, a research associate at the Inter-Hemispheric Education Resource Center, is the author, co-author, or contributor to several books, including *The Great Divide: The Challenge of U.S.-Mexico Relations in the 1990s*, *Runaway America: U.S. Jobs and Factories on the Move*, *Workers of the World Undermined: American Labor's Role in U.S. Foreign Policy* (South End Press, 1992), and *Mexico: A Country Guide* (Resource Center, 1992). She received her Master's in Political Science from the University of New Mexico.

Resource
Center
Press

Resource Center Press is the imprint of the Inter-Hemispheric Education Resource Center, a private, non-profit, research and policy institute located in Albuquerque, New Mexico. Founded in 1979, the Resource Center produces books, policy reports, audiovisuals, and other educational materials about U.S. foreign policy, as well as sponsoring popular education projects. For more information and a catalog of publications, please write to the Resource Center, Box 4506, Albuquerque, New Mexico 87196.

Board of Directors

Forthcoming from Grove Press, April 1994

The Great Divide

The Challenge of U.S.-Mexico Relations in the 1990s

Tom Barry, Harry Browne, and Beth Sims

"All international borders are at once fascinating and disconcerting . . . But it is not the contrasting cultures . . . that [make] crossing the U.S.-Mexico line so shocking . . . it is the experience of passing so rapidly between economic worlds.**"** — *excerpt*

The Great Divide is an in-depth examination of the U.S.-Mexico relationship—one that has often been volatile, characterized by prejudice, imperialism, and violence, and only recently by cooperation and mutual dependence. This precarious harmony is threatened by the potentially problematic ramifications of the North American Free Trade Agreement, which, if passed, promises to change permanently the nature of the relationship.

Bound as the U.S. and Mexico are by trade, debt, immigration, and the drug war, the economic and social issues that face both countries play out most visibly along the border. Nine thousand people a day cross illegally into the U.S. through the borderlands; 2,000 maquiladora factories spread across the borderlands employ nearly 500,000 Mexicans and yet are subject to virtually no labor or environmental laws; 50 percent of the cocaine and 75 percent of the marijuana smuggled into the U.S. comes through the borderlands; and the pollution in the area is so bad that a section of the Nogales Wash, a borderlands river, recently exploded.

This is another book in the Grove Press series which includes *The Central America Fact Book* and *Central America Inside Out*.

Mexico: A Country Guide

*The Essential Source on Mexican Society,
Economy, and Politics*

Edited by Tom Barry

One of our best sellers, *Mexico: A Country Guide* is the only comprehensive book about Mexican society, politics, and economy in the 1990s—an invaluable resource for students, academics, and anyone interested in the interrelationship between our two countries. Includes photos, tables and charts, references, and index.

"Easily the best source book on contemporary Mexican society." – Choice: Current Reviews for College Libraries

ISBN: 0-911213-35-X
Paperback, 401 pages, 1992. $14.95
plus $3.00 shipping and handling

BorderLines

A quarterly from the Resource Center focusing on border issues

This quarterly is an extension of the Resource Center's work on its Cross-Border Links project. It examines the dynamics of cross-border relations, highlighting the problems and successes of popular organizations and government agencies in resolving common issues. It also offers investigative reporting and timely policy analysis about Mexico-U.S. relations.

U.S. subscriptions: $10/year, $17/2 years
Foreign subscriptions: $15/year, $27/2 years

Prices subject to change.

Resource Center
Box 4506 / Albuquerque, NM 87196
(505) 842-8288

The U.S.-Mexico Series

The Challenge of Cross-Border Environmentalism:
The U.S.-Mexico Case

Few predicted the clout environmentalists now have in international trade discussions. Suddenly, environmental issues have become central to the rapidly evolving relationship between the United States and Mexico. *The Challenge of Cross-Border Environmentalism* explores diverse environmental issues—including cross-border air and water contamination, pesticides, pollution-haven investment, maquiladora wastes, sharing of water resources, and impacts of liberalized trade—and examines how governments and citizen groups are responding to new environmental challenges. The book, copublished by the Resource Center Press and the Border Ecology Project, focuses on conditions in the U.S.-Mexico borderlands where many of these problems and challenges are most apparent.

No. 1 in the series. ISBN: 0-911213-45-7. 121 pages, paperback, $9.95

On Foreign Soil: Government Programs in U.S.-Mexico Relations

Disagreements and misunderstandings have traditionally characterized the U.S.-Mexico relationship. Since the mid-1980s, however, the two governments have increasingly seen eye to eye on issues ranging from economics to international affairs. Similar economy policy agendas—characterized by neoliberal policies and free trade initiatives—are the foundation of this new mutual understanding. But simmering beneath the improved relations are such intractable issues as immigration, labor mobility, narcotrafficking, economic disparities, and asymmetric trading and investment power. *On Foreign Soil* breaks new ground in examining current U.S.-Mexico foreign relations, while providing an investigative look at the government programs that characterize this fragile new partnership.

No. 2 in the series. ISBN: 0-911213-44-9. 84 pages, paperback, $9.95

For Richer, For Poorer: Shaping U.S.-Mexican Integration

Money and business are integrating North America. More than any other factor, they have brought the United States and Mexico closer together than at any time since the 1917 Mexican Revolution. The two countries' histories as leaders of the industrialized North and the developing South, respectively, make the emerging partnership a highly influential model for the rest of the world. Important sectors in both nations stand to benefit from closer integration, but the neoliberal economic policies that have cleared the way for booming cross-border trade and investment are wreaking havoc on workers, small businesses, and communities across the continent, and forcing people on both sides of the Rio Grande to come to grips with globalization for the first time. *For Richer, For Poorer* explains the nuts and bolts of globalization, the pros and cons of the free trade debate, and alternative strategies to promote a more balanced process of integration that advances workers' rights and the environment as well as business interests.

No. 4 in the series. ISBN: 0-911213-47-3. 130 pages, paperback, $9.95

**Include $3.00 shipping and handling for the first book,
50¢ for each additional. Prices subject to change.**

**Resource Center
Box 4506 / Albuquerque, NM 87196
(505) 842-8288**